WHY DO PEOPLE MIGRATE?

WHY DO PEOPLE MIGRATE?

Labour Market Security and Migration Decisions

Edited by

MACIEJ DUSZCZYK
University of Warsaw, Poland

United Kingdom – North America – Japan
India – Malaysia – China

Emerald Publishing Limited
Howard House, Wagon Lane, Bingley BD16 1WA, UK

First edition 2019

Editorial matter and selection Copyright © 2019
Maciej Duszczyk; individual chapters © the respective authors,
published under exclusive licence.

Reprints and permissions service
Contact: permissions@emeraldinsight.com

No part of this book may be reproduced, stored in a retrieval
system, transmitted in any form or by any means electronic,
mechanical, photocopying, recording or otherwise without
either the prior written permission of the publisher or a licence
permitting restricted copying issued in the UK by The Copyright
Licensing Agency and in the USA by The Copyright Clearance
Center. Any opinions expressed in the chapters are those of the
authors. Whilst Emerald makes every effort to ensure the quality
and accuracy of its content, Emerald makes no representation
implied or otherwise, as to the chapters' suitability and
application and disclaims any warranties, express or implied, to
their use.

British Library Cataloguing in Publication Data
A catalogue record for this book is available from the British
Library

ISBN: 978-1-83867-750-3 (Print)
ISBN: 978-1-83867-747-3 (Online)
ISBN: 978-1-83867-749-7 (EPub)

Printed and bound by CPI Group (UK) Ltd, Croydon, CR0 4YY

ISOQAR certified
Management System,
awarded to Emerald
for adherence to
Environmental
standard
ISO 14001:2004.

Certificate Number 1985
ISO 14001

INVESTOR IN PEOPLE

CONTENTS

About the Contributors   vii

Acknowledgement   ix

Introduction
   Maciej Duszczyk   1

1. Labour Market Security and Migration-related Decisions: Theoretical Background
   Maciej Duszczyk and Kamil Matuszczyk   25

2. Are the Countries Different? Statistical View on Labour Market Security
   Kamil Matuszczyk   67

3. Why and Where: Labour Market Security as a Push-pull Factor
   Maciej A. Górecki, Kamil Matuszczyk and Monika Stec   105

4. Migration Policy: Recommendations for Sending and Receiving Countries
   Maciej Duszczyk   131

5. Conclusions
   Maciej Duszczyk   147

Index   151

ABOUT THE CONTRIBUTORS

Maciej Duszczyk is based at the University of Warsaw, Poland, as Vice-Rector for Research, and is a member of the Board of Centre of Migration Research and the Transatlantic Forum on Migration and Integration. In 2008–2011, he was a member of the Board of Strategic Advisers to the Prime Minister of Poland.

Maciej A. Górecki is an Assistant Professor at the Faculty of Psychology, University of Warsaw. His main research interests are elections and voting. He has published articles in *Electoral Studies*, *European Journal of Political Research*, *International Journal of Public Opinion Research*, *Political Geography*, *Political Studies*, *Scandinavian Political Studies* and *West European Politics*.

Kamil Matuszczyk is a PhD candidate in the Faculty of Political Science and International Studies, and Research Assistant at Centre of Migration Research, University of Warsaw. His main research interests are labour migration, long-term care, ageing of society and social policy.

Monika Stec is a Sociologist and Qualitative Researcher (PhD studies in Graduate School for Social Research), since 2007 involved with social research on labour market, local communities, education, new technologies, discrimination, stereotypes and prejudices. Her main research interests are discourse analysis, social innovations, methodology of qualitative research and ethics in research.

ACKNOWLEDGEMENT

This book is an output of the research project 'In Search of Labour Market Security. Migration to and from Poland and the Attractiveness of the Polish Labour Market', financed by the Polish National Centre of Science within the framework of the OPUS programme (contract UMO-2014/15/B/HS5/01148).

INTRODUCTION
Maciej Duszczyk

INTRODUCTION

The twentieth century is oftentimes referred to as 'the century of migration' (e.g. Castles, de Haas, & Miller, 2014). In the second half of it, the migration status of many countries had gradually changed; they had evolved from being typical countries of emigration to acquiring the status of countries of both emigration and immigration, to have eventually become countries of immigration. In Europe, the greatest transformation in that sphere had taken place in countries of the south of the continent, that is, in Italy, Spain, Portugal, Ireland and Greece. They had thus been named 'new countries of immigration' (Okólski, 2012). At the same time, countries of Central and Eastern Europe, in spite of their having been open to immigration as a result of the systemic transformation that started in 1989, retained their status of typical countries of emigration. The initial period of their membership in the European Union (EU), joined by most of those countries in 2004, brought no change in this respect. The magnitude of the wave of post-accession migration has undoubtedly exceeded the relevant forecasts (Boeri & Brücker, 2000; Fassmann & Hintermann, 1997; Wallace, 1998). It has perhaps actually been one of the many causes of the current political crisis in the EU. The result of the Brexit referendum having been the most adverse effect it co-determined. Anyway, it was not until the second decade of the twenty-first century that the migration status of the countries of Central Europe changed, with great numbers of citizens of Ukraine starting to flow in and settle throughout the region (see Duszczyk & Matuszczyk, 2016). This was related to the deteriorating economic situation in Ukraine, a result of delayed free-market reforms, as well as to the socio-economic consequences of the armed conflict in the east of the country. Owing to the mass influx of Ukrainians and, on a smaller scale, migrants from other East European countries, Central European states have rapidly transformed into emigration-immigration settings.

Poland has been the country facing most pronounced change of migration status. The number of foreigners to whom temporary residence permits were issued grew dramatically in the years 2014–2018, from below 40,000 in 2014 to over 200,000 in 2018. There was a similar increase in permanent residence permits within the same period, their number having increased from 25,000 to 67,000 (Office for Foreigners, 2019). At the same time, a dynamic growth of the numbers of foreigners in the Polish labour market occurred, especially with respect to the segment of seasonal jobs. Within just the three-year period between 2015 and 2018, the respective figures increased by over 300% (Ministry of Family, Labour and Social Policy, 2019). During that time, for many Ukrainian nationals, Poland became a destination rather than just a transition country. Notably, all the aforementioned large-scale shifts have brought about neither an increase in unemployment rates nor a drop of employment figures in Poland. It caused no major social tensions either (Duszczyk & Matuszczyk, 2018). The increase in the attractiveness of Poland for immigrants is largely confirmed by the Eurostat data on the scale of first residence permits issued in the EU countries in 2015–2017. For instance, in 2017 for

Poland, the number amounted to more than 683,000, well above the numbers recorded for some of the typical countries of immigration, such as Germany (535,000) or the United Kingdom (517,000); (Eurostat, 2019).

Regardless of the emergence of Poland as an attractive destination setting for migrants from the East of Europe, the number of Poles residing in those EU member states that have traditionally been destinations for emigrants has not dropped. In 2014, about 1,800,000 Poles were living in countries of the 'old EU', and in 2017 that number even rose by 200,000. It is estimated that at the end of 2017 2,540,000 Poles were living outside their native country. The leading destination countries for Polish emigrants remain unchanged and include the United Kingdom, Germany, the Netherlands and Ireland (The Central Statistical Office, 2018). In spite of the improving macroeconomic situation in Poland, in 2017, about 13% of Poles interviewed were still considering the possibility of emigration. Unsurprisingly, they mentioned the attractiveness of the labour markets of the EU-15 countries, in addition to difficulties finding high-quality employment in Poland, as major factors that spur emigration (Work Service, 2017).

All the aforementioned data sources indicate that Poland is facing an increasing presence of foreigners, especially in the labour market, while, at the same time, being a country where emigration is still holding up. It can thus be classified as having the status of an emigration-immigration country. While such a situation is not unusual in the history of migration – Spain and Italy mentioned here, had gone through the same phase in their migration history – the speed of that process in the case of Poland is exceptional, especially as regards immigration.

The dynamic transformation of Poland and, more broadly, Central Europe into an emigration-immigration context raises new research questions and can potentially facilitate the study of some phenomena that would otherwise pose enormous difficulties to the scholarly community. Among others, it includes research that can potentially make an additional contribution to theories of migration and provide a better explanation of the migrations taking place in Europe and beyond. The factors determining individual-level migration-related decisions would certainly be one of the topics which such research could throw new light on. Although there does exist an extensive literature analysing the factors 'pushing' and 'pulling' immigrants, there are still many shortcomings suffered by the theories explaining the highly complex processes of making migration-related decisions. The relevant extant literature has thus far tended to be dominated by theoretical perspectives emphasising broadly conceived economic aspects, such as salaries, costs of living and access to health services, political factors, such as regulation of migration, and, finally, social ones, including social/migration networks.

The present publication is part of a scholarly debate that attempts to explain why only a part of the population makes decisions to look for employment in countries other than their native one. In particular, we are interested in establishing whether or not labour market security, broadly conceived, is one of the factors behind migrants' decisions of leaving their country of origin and whether or not if affects their choice of destination countries. We understand 'labour market security' as the ability to gain and maintain employment which allows the fulfilment of one's objectives, that is, income security. This can be achieved in various ways. For example, an immigrant may feel 'secure' if, following losing a job, he/she can be employed again in a short time. In such a situation, an individual may value employment mobility and perceive 'security' as determined by his/her own skills and professional experience. He/she is thus confident that losing employment is not a disaster as he/she can find another job very quickly. In this case, 'flexible' forms of employment may be viewed as attractive. In an alternative scenario, an individual feels secure due to the possibility of retaining the job once he/she has got it. There are many factors driving that kind of 'security'. For instance, the individual ensures retaining employment by improving his/her own professional qualifications. At the same time, he/she may expect labour law to be designed in such a way as to make laying off employees difficult for employers. We should assume that for individuals holding such an attitude, the labour markets offering advanced systems of employee protection will be most attractive. Applying the terms used in the extant literature on labour markets, we can refer to the former model as emphasising 'employment security', while the other one can tend to put greater weight on 'job security' (see Esser & Olsen, 2012; Marx, 2014; Matuszczyk & Duszczyk, 2018).

In order to answer the question as to whether or not labour market security is relevant for making decisions to emigrate, and, if so, whether or not the expectations concerning the ways to achieve it determine the choice of the country of destination, comparative empirical research project has been carried out. The results from the project are presented in this publication.[1] In addition to interviews with experts on migration, the empirics of the project are based on a social survey Paper and Pen Personal Interview (PAPI) and qualitative (in-depth) interviews with labour migrants. Our respondents and interviewees were recruited mostly from among Poles employed in the United Kingdom and Germany for at least 12 months and Ukrainians living and working in Poland for 12 months or longer. This time perspective made it possible to examine how experience gained by the migrants in a particular country translates, among other things, into conditions of employment, the migrants' knowledge of public institutions and perceptions of different dimensions of labour-related security. In other words, we set out to establish to what extent experience of a destination country affects the level of security in the labour market. Furthermore, we attempt to examine whether or not it brings about changes in the preferred model of security, shifting the preference from a model based on employment security in favour of the one based on job security or vice versa.

The theoretical foundations of the presented monograph are constituted mainly by Lee's (1966) model of making migration-related decisions, based on identification of push-pull factors. The model was repeatedly criticised but equally often defended (King, 2012). Critics pointed to its taking neo-classic approach, most notably assuming that migrants are rational in their decisions and have adequate knowledge of the situation in the country they are leaving and in the country of their destination. Such an idealised situation indeed occurs quite rarely. Nonetheless, those defending Lee's theory have emphasised that it helps us to explain the fundamental determinants of migration decisions and to understand which factors, and in what order of importance, are taken into consideration by a potential migrant. We are thus certainly aware of major shortcomings of the concept, especially the aforementioned assumption that a person analysing the push-pull factors has adequate knowledge to make a rational decision. In practice, this might never be the case. However, the present-day development of migration networks and access to social networks allow migrants to gain a much greater knowledge than in the past. Therefore, the 'push and pull' theory is currently being 'rediscovered' by migration researchers. It was selected by authors of this monograph also because it seems to suit ideally the task of examining security on the labour market as a migration-related factor. In the case of expected security, we deal exactly with attitudes and views before departure, updated following the commencement of one's employment in the receiving state. Thus, it can be assumed that the possibility of gaining security in the labour market of the receiving state is perceived as a pull factor, while the absence of this type of security in the state of origin is a push factor.

It should be emphasised at the outset that the extant literature has not paid due attention to the problem of labour market security in the context of factors influencing various kinds of migration-related decisions. The literature trying to explain this sort of decisions has thus far tended to focus on factors such as disparities in salaries, demand on part of employers or functioning of migration networks (Dustmann & Glitz, 2005; Hatton & Williamson, 2005; Kahanec, Zaiceva, & Zimmermann, 2010; Kennan & Walker, 2013). At the same time, decisions concerning employment, emigration and settling abroad are undoubtedly more complex than a simple calculus based solely on the aforementioned security considerations. Therefore, the main hypothesis of the project constitutes a partial explanation only, acknowledging the fact that the security of the labour market is merely one of the co-determinants of migration-related decisions, albeit an important one, operating jointly with factors such as salary levels or the supply of jobs.

Labour market security should be taken into consideration when asking questions regarding both the decision to emigrate and the choice of the country of destination. It also certainly affects the situation of the emigrant in a particular labour market. In spite of the development of legislation regulating the issues of labour market and social policy at the level of the entire European Community, there still are differences among the EU member states with respect to regulation of the domains such as labour relations, social security systems or the various state-funded benefits which both the unemployed and the employees are entitled to (e.g. family income supplements, housing benefits). There are a number of studies classifying countries into groups characterised by different models of social policy and labour market regulations. The initial scholarly exploration of those different social models took place as early as the first half of the sixties of the twentieth century. The models were distinguished according to the share of social expenditures in a country's gross national income (Golinowska, 2018). A more nuanced approach was initiated by Titmus (1974) in the early 1970s. Based on an analysis of the relations between social policy and free-market economic policy, he distinguished three models. The first, or the marginal one, assumes the accomplishment of the desired state of social security in the labour market through individual resourcefulness with little regulation or intervention on part of the state. Under the second, motivational model, the universality of social insurance is conditioned by the amount of premiums paid. It incentivizes active participation in the labour market but, at the same time, offers benefits in case of unemployment and in other legitimate instances of dropping out of the labour market. Finally the institutional-distributional model assumes that work is a value but it nonetheless offers general access to the system of social welfare based on one's needs, making it possible to gain security also outside the labour market.

Another scholar who contributed greatly to our understanding of the variety of social models is Esping-Andersen (1990). In the early 1990s he suggested new criteria for assigning states to a particular social model and put forward a new classification of those models. He distinguished three types of those: liberal, conservative-corporate and social-democratic. At the beginning of the twenty-first century, Sapir (2005) proposed a yet another typology, designed for the purpose of a debate within the EU. His typology is based on two essential criteria: the rate of employment and the rate of poverty. Relying on indices capturing the aforementioned criteria, he distinguished four social models within the then EU-15. The four models are referred to as, respectively, continental (Austria, Belgium, France, Germany and Luxembourg), Scandinavian (Denmark Finland, Sweden and the Netherlands), Mediterranean (Greece, Italy, Portugal and Spain) and Anglo-Saxon (Ireland and the United Kingdom).

'Varieties of capitalism' (VoC) is yet another theory on the basis of which we can make a breakdown of states in terms of the models they apply to guarantee labour market security (Dixon, Fullerton, & Robertson, 2013; Hall & Soskice, 2001). In accordance with that theory, national economies differ with respect to a number of crucial characteristics, including the modes in which firms acquire capital, the role of formal contracting and so on. On the basis of those differences, we can distinguish two 'ideal types' of capitalist economies: liberal market economies (LMEs) and coordinated market economies (CMEs). In the former type of economy, labour market security tends to prevail in labour relations, while the latter one creates circumstances for the emergence of job security as a predominant model (see more in Chapter 3).

It should be emphasised that nowadays the typologies mentioned here represent ideal, theoretical types of social models. Various policies implemented at the turn of the twentieth and twenty-first centuries have caused the blurring of the initially sharp differences between these models. A good example here is, for instance, the policy of flexicurity promoted by the European Commission, constituting a hybrid approach unrepresented in the aforementioned typologies.

Looking at both the above-mentioned socio-economic models practiced by the EU member states and the destinations of Polish emigrants following Poland's accession to the EU in 2004, we notice that Poles tended to choose countries differing substantially as regards regulations applied in the labour market and thereby the represented models of social policy. Germany and the United Kingdom are the countries topping the list of those that receive the greatest numbers of labour immigrants from Poland. Curiously, those two states represent radically different approaches to regulating labour relations. Using the terminology proposed by Sapir, Germany is a country of the continental model while the United Kingdom represents the Anglo-Saxon one (if we take to account theory of 'varieties of capitalism' United Kingdom represents LME and Germany CME). This means that in Germany the regulations in force concerning the labour market are extensive, with the state claiming the right to intervene in the relations between the employers and the employees, most usually in order to protect the rights of the latter. Simplifying to a certain extent, we can say that labour market security there is accomplished through job security. Those participating in workforce tend to get and maintain employment with a single employer for a longer period of time. In the case of the United Kingdom, on the contrary, the regulations concerning the labour market are much more flexible. Except for the most obvious cases, such as violating workers' fundamental rights, the state does not intervene in the relations between the employers and the employees. Even if a worker performs his/her work well, he/she can be laid off relatively easily. But, however, he/she is not bound by any restrictions preventing him/her from changing employers. Employers' relative freedom of laying off workforce is thus partly counterbalanced by workers' relative freedom to undertake a job with a more 'attractive' employer. As a result, employers do not need to be anxious to increase the number of staff they hire in times of prosperity as they are aware that they will be able to make quick 'adjustments' in times of a downturn. At the same time, they may need to be able to offer attractive conditions of employment, since, in accordance with the regulations, a worker faces no great legal obstacles in quitting a job and looking for another employer. All in all, this means that, unlike with Germany, in the case of the United Kingdom, labour market security is accomplished through employment security.

When trying to evaluate the social models adopted by Central and Eastern European countries in accordance with the aforementioned classifications, we encounter a number of difficulties. Neither Esping-Andersen nor Sapir nor Hall and Soskice referred directly to those countries; they focused almost exclusively on the so-called 'old' EU member states. In recent years, however, a number of single-country studies have been published. The authors of those tried to name and describe the social model of a given country from the region of Central and Eastern Europe. When it comes to the Polish-language literature, such attempts were made by, among others, Duszczyk (2008) and Golinowska (2018). For the Central and Eastern European countries, both these authors pointed to the need of distinguishing a unique social model that emerged in the course of transformation from the centrally planned economy to a free-market one. Regarding the social model in operation in Poland, we should point out that it was reformed comprehensively following the collapse of state socialism in 1989. The overarching principle of those reforms was getting rid of the so-called 'socialist welfare state' (Golinowska, 2018). In the period of 30 years since the beginning of the transformation, different sorts of reforms have been implemented. Depending on the party being in office at a given time, the particular solutions implemented drew on the experiences of either the continental model or its Anglo-Saxon counterpart. Although the Polish Constitution, introduced in 1997, states unequivocally that the economy functioning in Poland is 'the social market economy', the actual principles guiding labour relations tend to be of a liberal character. It is so especially if we consider the relative prevalence of the so-called 'flexible forms of employment'. In effect, we are dealing with a hybrid social model, combining different, oftentimes contradictory, approaches to social policy as well as forms of labour market regulation. Moreover, the labour market is 'segmented', with the participants of the particular 'segments' being offered radically different types of contracts and thereby enjoying (suffering) drastically different levels of security.

With regard to Ukraine, it is extremely difficult to ascertain which social model prevails. Since 1990, the year the country gained independence, no meaningful social or economic changes have been introduced. A high level of corruption and a nepotistic job placement system hinder the evaluation of the mechanisms through which labour market security can be accomplished in that country. Simplifying to a certain extent, we can say that security can be gained solely by means of joining the group of the privileged who, through the network of contacts and mutual exchange of 'favours', can guarantee both gaining and maintaining employment and thereby income security. The Ukrainian model thus essentially deviates from all the models known in the EU member states. This allows the assumption that the lack of stability and the deprivation of fundamental rights in the labour market in Ukraine, resulting from informal practices of employers, employees as well as public institutions, can be important factors pushing people out of that country.

When it comes to characterizing the countries of destination for Polish migrants in terms of the social models implemented across the EU, we can come to the conclusion that individuals who strongly believe in their own qualifications and other work-related qualities, in addition to being willing to accept risk, will tend to choose the United Kingdom with its model that incentivizes frequent switching of jobs. They would tend to be open to changing employers often and accept short periods of unemployment they would spend on searching for more rewarding jobs. They are primarily younger workers with relatively little professional experience. More conservative and risk-averse persons, viewing their labour market security as maintaining their job and thus being reluctant to accept periods of unemployment, will rather choose Germany with its regulations designed to assure employment stability. This group of people will comprise mainly the older, more experienced workers who have families and for whom stability is an important element in their migration plans.

With regard to migration from Ukraine to Poland, the situation is somewhat different. It can be assumed that Ukrainians decide to take employment in Poland mainly because of the extraordinarily harsh labour market situation in their own country and the related lack of opportunities which would allow for an acceptable level of security. They are aware that in Poland they have to rely mainly on their own skills, especially on the ability of adapting to the changing requirements on part of the employers. They have also to accept remaining in the 'grey zone' of the labour market, a 'zone' dominated by illegal or semi-legal jobs, or working only on fixed-term employment contracts. They thus can gain security solely through employment security. Importantly, their situation is different from that of Poles in the United Kingdom or in Germany. The fundamental difference is that Poles in the EU member states can take advantage of the right of free movement of workers between the EU countries, which guarantees numerous entitlements, while Ukrainians in Poland are subject to Polish immigration regulations only.

Those regulations restrict rights of foreigners, including the length of the time of employment and stay as well as access to the social security system.

The issues raised in this introduction are multidimensional. Not only do they include the factors explaining migration-related decisions, but they also encompass the perspectives of different categories of workers: the citizens of the EU (the Poles) who look for employment and work on labour markets of the EU member states (United Kingdom and Germany) as well as the citizens of a third country (the Ukrainians) coming to one of the EU member states in order to take up employment. Such an approach will allow for a more nuanced study of the issue of labour market security and its role in making migration-related decisions. Moreover, it should limit the risk of drawing conclusions based entirely on partial analyses.

The monograph consists of an introduction, final conclusions and four chapters. The first chapter by Maciej Duszczyk and Kamil Matuszczyk presents theoretical and methodological assumptions applied in the research project. The main part of it contains a review of literature of the topics of labour market security and the making of migration-related decisions. Based on an in-depth analysis of the literature, the research gap in the area of the relationship between the making of migration-related decisions and labour market security is identified. At the same time, this chapter enables the reader to take a closer look at the complexity of the concept of labour market security and the particular elements of this approach, applied in the research on individual subjective assessments of functioning in the labour market (job security, income security, employment security). Different analytic approaches reflecting the situation of labour migrants in the receiving countries – among others, the 'precarious' migration and welfare migration – are as well presented. Explaining the difference between the two approaches to labour market security is of key importance. The authors term one of them 'employment security', based on the assumption that a migrant's preferred notion of security and the related choice of a labour market stem from him/her being convinced that a potential loss of a job will shortly be followed by finding another one. They also distinguish the other approach, 'job security', based on the assumption that a particular migrant looks for a country of destination which offers stability of work, often guaranteed by the regulations of the respective Labour Code. Literature of the topic has been analysed in these terms. Based on these concepts, new theoretical foundations for studying labour market security are presented, going far beyond the welfare magnet hypothesis (Borjas, 1999; Kureková, 2013). In that chapter, the authors also refer to the labour market segmentation theory (Lee, 1966), analysing the potential obstacles to the access to labour market institutions and to equal access to various types of job offers.

In Chapter 2, Kamil Matuszczyk presents a comparative analysis of labour markets in Poland, the United Kingdom, Germany and Ukraine, with a special focus on the issue of labour market security, including the prevalent social models. Basic macroeconomic indicators (e.g. unemployment rate, employment rate, average income), defining the overall situation on the labour markets, have been relied on. Based on a review of literature, Eurostat databases, Organisation for Economic Co-operation and Development (OECD) databases and Employment Protection Legislation Index, the main features characterizing social models in the selected countries are identified. The analyses also exploit the data collected by international comparative survey programs (the European Social Survey, the European Working Conditions Survey and others), which show workers' subjective evaluations of labour markets. Some attention is also paid to the principal solutions and instruments regulating the situation of labour migrants in the countries studied. The review of the most important regulations of social law and labour market policy in the selected countries helps us to better understand the determinants that affect the levels of labour market security. He points to the differences between particular solutions from the viewpoint of the social models distinguished. The chapter aims to show the diversity in the level of labour market security. In this context, it is of key importance to answer the question about the extent to which the model of the labour market adopted by the countries analysed facilitates the accomplishment of labour market security through either 'employment security' or 'job security'. According to theories of social models, such as those put forward by Esping-Andersen and Sapir, the British and the German labour markets represent two divergent models: the continental and the Anglo-Saxon one. The author assumes that, more often than not, the British labour market will be chosen by persons searching for 'employment security', while those looking for 'job security' will tend to choose the German labour market. In the case of Ukraine, it was possible to perform only limited comparative studies. This followed mainly from absence of relevant statistical data. At the same time, it was possible to demonstrate that the model applied in Ukraine departs significantly from those typical of EU states.

Chapter 3, co-authored by Maciej A. Górecki, Kamil Matuszczyk and Monika Stec, presents the results of empirical, quantitative and qualitative research on attitudes of two categories of people: Poles working in Germany and Poles working in the United Kingdom. These are states which represent different labour market models in terms of security and graduates of Polish universities who were planning to leave Poland (most usually for Germany and the United Kingdom). In addition, outcomes of interviews with experts and scholars studying migration are presented, focusing on the role of labour market security in the context of migration policy. The authors conclude that the issue of labour market security is taken into consideration by those making migration decisions, especially when it comes to choosing the country of destination. At the same time, the importance of that factor is arguably limited. The expected pay in the receiving country, the availability of existing migration networks as well as the distance from the country of origin seem to prevail as determinants of migration decisions. Nonetheless, the results of the study indicate that there is a statistically significant correlation between a migrant's profile and his/her choice of the country of destination. Younger and better-educated individuals, and those confident that they are valuable and desirable workers, tend to choose the United Kingdom rather than Germany as their destination. Those who are older, often with a family to support and with less education, tend to prefer the German labour market with its exceptionally high standards of labour protection. Furthermore, Poles who have had an experience of both the British and the German labour markets tended to perceive either of those as superior in terms of labour market security to the Polish labour market. Similarly, Ukrainians who had worked in Poland had a higher opinion of the Polish labour market than of that in Ukraine. Curiously, however, the disparity in favour of Poland in the Ukrainians' evaluations was considerably smaller than the corresponding difference in the evaluations of Poles comparing the Polish labour market to those of, respectively, Germany and Britain.

Chapter 4 authored by Maciej Duszczyk summarises the results of empirical research with regard to the shaping of migration policies in particular countries. The author attempts to establish in what way the social model applied by a particular country, including the scope and type of labour market security, can promote immigration or emigration. Duszczyk believes this is an important adjustment to one of the most prominent migration theories, that is, the concept of 'push and pull factors' (Lee, 1966). Moreover, recommendations are worked out for the migration policies of particular states in the context of labour market security issues. Although an overwhelmingly large part of the research discussed here focused on migrations within the EU, that is, within the framework of a free movement of workers, its results nevertheless allow drawing conclusions about migration policy in general. This includes recommendations for potential changes in the immigration-related domains of labour market regulation. This part also contains recommendations for civil servants responsible for designing migration policies and for managing migration. The author assumes that the regulations introduced may influence the profiles of immigrants willing to be participants of particular labour markets. Therefore, countries interested in attracting immigrants accepting the necessity of changing jobs frequently, but also loosely connected with the local labour market, should apply flexible solutions, that is, ones that allow immigrants to change jobs relatively often. This means, for instance, that the potential work permit issued to residents of a third country, arriving from outside the EU, should not include any rigid connection between an employer and an employee, meaning that following a loss of a job an immigrant should leave the receiving country. On the contrary, immigrants should have the right to repeated switching between employers during their stay. Countries interested in attracting workers who would like to be connected to one employer permanently or for a longer period of time should draft regulations which would make the right to enter the country and to get a residence permit for citizens of third countries conditional on being offered long-term employment.

Thus, the loss of the job should entail an order to leave the receiving country. Such a model involves greater control by the state over the process of immigration. The scope of responsibility of employers is increasing as well. In this chapter, two perspectives are presented: that of the immigrants and that of the state. In the former case, the issue of labour market security is theorized as a factor behind individual migration-related decisions and the choice of a particular country of destination. In the latter one, that is, the one taking the perspective of the state, it is the element of migration policy, involving selective acceptance of immigrants mediated by both the demand for work on part of the economy and the model of immigration adopted by a given country.

In the final part, Maciej Duszczyk summarises the project by presenting the results arrived at in its course. The conclusion refers in particular to labour market security as a factor co-determining migration-related decisions and the choice of the country of destination. The 'push and pull' theory is very dynamic and it should be assumed that with the development of new models of employment within the 4.0 economy (post-Fordism), also the factors relevant for making migration-related decisions will be evolving rapidly. For example, will, anytime in the foreseeable future, the issue of services at a distance affect the migration processes to a greater extent than it does nowadays?

The authors cherish the hope that the results of research discussed in this publication will facilitate a better understanding of the factors behind the decisions to migrate as well as the directions of migrations. This knowledge can be used in creating migration policies of respective countries. It hopefully has value not only from the viewpoint of basic research but also from the perspective of applied science. We thus hope that this publication meets with interest on part of both the scholarly community and political decision-maker.

NOTE

1. The results presented in this book are an output of the research project: 'In Search of Labour Market Security. Migration to and from Poland and the Attractiveness of the Polish Labour Market', financed by the Polish National Centre of Science within the framework of the OPUS programme (contract UMO-2014/15/B/HS5/01148).

REFERENCES

Boeri, T., & Brücker, H. (2000). The impact of Eastern enlargement on employment and labour markets in the EU member states. Retrieved from http://www.frdb.org/be/file/_scheda/files/ec_exsumm_1_5.pdf

Borjas, G. J. (1999). Immigration and welfare magnets. *Journal of Labor Economics*, *17*(4), 607−637.

Castles, S., de Haas, H., & Miller, M. J. (2014). *The age of migration. International population movements in the modern world (Fifth ed.)*. Basingstoke: Palgrave Macmillan.

Dixon, J. C., Fullerton, A. S., & Robertson, D. L. (2013). Cross-national differences in workers' perceived job, labour market, and employment insecurity in Europe: Empirical tests and theoretical extensions. *European Sociological Review*, *29*(5), 1053−1067. doi:10.1093/esr/jcs084

Dustmann, Ch., & Glitz, A. (2005). *Immigration, jobs and wages: Theory, evidence and opinion*. London: Centre for Economic Policy Research.

Duszczyk, M. (2008). Wyzwania polityki migracyjnej a doświadczenia międzynarodowe. In P. Kaczmarczyk & M. Okólski (Eds.), *Polityka migracyjna jako instrument promocji zatrudnienia i ograniczania bezrobocia* (pp. 11–20). Warszawa: Ośrodek Badań nad Migracjami WNE Uniwersytet Warszawski.

Duszczyk, M., & Matuszczyk, K. (2016). *The beginning of the end. Will the migrants cause the EU to collapse?* Warsaw: Central and Eastern Europe Development Institute.

Duszczyk, M., & Matuszczyk, K. (2018). The employment of foreigners in Poland and the labour market situation. *Central and Eastern European Migration Review*, 7(2), 53–68. doi:10.17467/ceemr.2018.07

Esping-Andersen, G. (1990). *The three worlds of welfare capitalism.* Cambridge: Polity Press.

Esser, I., & Olsen, K. M. (2012). Perceived job quality: Autonomy and job security within a multi-level framework. *European Sociological Review*, 28(4), 443–454. doi:10.1093/esr/jcr009

Eurostat. (2019). First permits by reason, length of validity and citizenship [migr_resfirst]. Retrieved from http://appsso.eurostat.ec.europa.eu/nui/show.do?dataset=migr_resfirst&lang=en

Fassmann, H., & Hintermann, C. (1997). Migrationspotential Ostmitteleuropa. Struktur und Motivation potentieller Migranten aus Polen, der Slowakei, Tschechien und Ungarn, ISR – Forschungsberichte, *Institut für Stadt-und Regionalforschung*. Retreived from https://www.oeaw.ac.at/fileadmin/Institute/ISR/pdf/publications/fb15.pdf

Golinowska, S. (2018). *Modele polityki społecznej w Polsce i Europie na początku XXI wieku.* Warszawa: Fundacja Batorego.

Hall, P. A., & Soskice, D. (2001). *Varieties of capitalism: The institutional foundations of comparative advantage.* Oxford: Oxford University Press.

Hatton, T. J., & Williamson, J. G. (2005). *Global migration and the world economy. Two centuries of policy and performance.* Cambridge, MA: MIT Press.

Kahanec, M., Zaiceva, A., & Zimmermann, K. F. (2010). Lessons from migration after EU enlargement. In M. Kahanec & K. F. Zimmermann (Eds.), *EU labour markets after post-enlargement migration* (pp. 3–45). Bonn: Springer Verlag.

Kennan, J., & Walker, J. R. (2013). Modelling individual migration decisions. In A. Constant & K. Zimmermann (Eds.), *The international handbook of the economics of migration.* Northampton: Edward Elgar Publishing.

King, R. (2012). Theories and typologies of migration: An review and a primer. Willy Brandt series of working papers in International Migration and Ethnic Relations. Retrieved from https://www.mah.se/upload/Forskningscentrum/MIM/WB/WB%203.12.pdf

Kureková, L. (2013). Welfare systems as emigration factor. Evidence from the new accession states. *Journal of Common Market Studies, 51*(4), 721–739. doi:10.1111/jcms.12020

Lee, E. (1966). A theory of migration. *Demography, 3*(1), 47–57.

Marx, P. (2014). The effect of job insecurity and employability on preferences for redistribution in Western Europe. *Journal of European Social Policy, 24*(4), 351–366. doi:10.1177/0958928714538217

Matuszczyk, K., & Duszczyk, M. (2018). Bezpieczeństwo na rynku pracy jako perspektywa teoretyczna w badaniach nad migracjami zarobkowymi. *Problemy Polityki Społecznej. Studia i Dyskusje*, 43(4), 25–42.

Ministry of Family, Labour and Social Policy. (2019). Cudzoziemcy pracujący w Polsce – statystyki. Retrieved from https://archiwum.mpips.gov.pl/analizy-i-raporty/cudzoziemcy-pracujacy-w-polsce-statystyki/

Office for Foreigners. (2019). Polska/Aktualne dokumenty/Wykresy/Porównanie lat 2018/2014. Retrieved from https://migracje.gov.pl/statystyki/zakres/polska/typ/dokumenty/widok/wykresy/rok/2018/rok2/2014

Okólski, M. (2012). Introduction. In M. Okólski (Ed.), *European immigrations. Trends, structures and policy implications* (pp. 7–22). Amsterdam: Amsterdam University Press.

Sapir, A. (2005). Globalisation and the reform of European social model. Bruegel. Retrieved from http://bruegel.org/wp-content/uploads/imported/publications/pc_sept2005_socialmod.pdf

The Central Statistical Office. (2018). Informacja o rozmiarach i kierunkach czasowej emigracji z Polski w latach 2004–2017. Retrieved from https://stat.gov.pl/obszary-tematyczne/ludnosc/migracje-zagraniczne-ludnosci/informacja-o-rozmiarach-i-kierunkach-czasowej-emigracji-z-polski-w-latach-2004–2017,2,11.html

Titmuss, R. (1974). Social policy. In B. Abel-Smith & K. Titmuss (Eds.), *An introduction*. New York, NY: Pantheon Press.

Wallace, C. (1998). *Migration potential in Central and Eastern Europe*. Geneva: International Organization for Migration.

Work Service. (2017). Migracje zarobkowe Polaków VII, Listopad 2017. Retrieved from http://www.workservice.com/pl/Centrum-prasowe/Raporty/Raport-Migracyjny/Migracje-Zarobkowe-Polakow-VII-listopad-2017

CHAPTER 1

LABOUR MARKET SECURITY AND MIGRATION-RELATED DECISIONS: THEORETICAL BACKGROUND

Maciej Duszczyk and Kamil Matuszczyk

INTRODUCTION

The dynamically changing labour market conditions, resulting from both the cyclical economic upturns and downturns and the evolution of global capitalism, bring the issues of finding and maintaining employment to the forefront. For most of us, gaining an appropriate employment is a key precondition for reaching the state of income security. At the same time, advanced industrial democracies, such as the EU member states, offer varying levels of protection through the system of social welfare and thereby supplement the security one can get through labour market. This allows for maintaining a certain standard of living when one is either out of employment for a relatively short period of time or permanently professionally passive, for example, because of reaching retirement age. The aforementioned are the elements constituting labour market security, meant as the condition of comfort for fulfilling the essential needs, both the individual ones and those of the other members of one's household. In search for conditions facilitating the accomplishment of this sort of security, some people resort to leaving their native country and emigrating elsewhere.

The goal of this chapter is to explain the essence of labour market security and its potential impact on migration-related decisions. The authors put forward a thesis that employment-related security is a vital factor affecting both individual decisions to migrate and the choice of destination of migration. Special attention has been paid to the concept of 'push-pull factors' which, even if often criticised, allows us to understand the significance of labour market security as one of the determinants of the process of making migration decisions. The chapter is of theoretical character; it discusses and comments on the main concepts appearing in the literature on the issues of labour market security. Based on the extant literature review, several avenues for further research have been identified. They have thus far been either overlooked or discussed only sparingly. It particularly concerns the different forms of gaining and maintaining labour market security, including emigration as a means of accomplishing it. Special emphasis has been put on the issue of reaching income security, which is the main dimension of labour market security. There are two approaches to this issue. One of them is based on the notion of job security, that is, a preference for gaining income security by finding a job and maintaining it for a longer time. The other emphasises employment security, that is, an acceptance of the possibility of frequent changes of employer, provided that intervals between employments are short and have no negative effect on income security. The problem of precarious employment, one of the dangers for labour market security, has also been referred to in this chapter. This threat is directly related to the processes of migration. Oftentimes, migrants undertake employment within the so-called secondary segment of the respective labour market, a segment in which gaining labour market security tends to be very difficult. Last but not least, the chapter also deals with a number of other issues, including labour protection legislation and the role of institutional and welfare state models.

LABOUR MARKET SECURITY AS A PRECONDITION OF THE ACCOMPLISHMENT OF INDIVIDUAL AND COLLECTIVE GOALS

In the era of post-Fordism, the character of labour relations has changed substantially (Edgell, 2006). The relative position of employees and the conditions of employment, in addition to the shape of the trajectories of professional careers, have undergone a far-reaching transformation. The fundamental institutions of the welfare state, which for decades guaranteed high standards of protection and labour market security, have been undergoing deep changes (Gardawski, Bartkowski, Męcina, & Czarzasty, 2010). Numerous essential workers' rights and privileges, secured under the framework of the postwar welfare state, are taking on a new essence in the time of high 'flexibilisation' of work. As Kiersztyn (2018, p. 93) notes, we are presently dealing with an intensification of both objective aspects of insecurity, determined by changes of the conditions of employment, and its subjective dimension, including feelings of threat and instability in the labour market. Heery and Salmon (2000, p. 2) summarise the changes as follows:

> *Employment in the developed economies has become more insecure or unstable in the sense that both continued employment and the level of remuneration have become less predictable and contingent on factors which lie beyond the employee's control.*

The turn of the twentieth and twenty-first centuries was the time of the fundamental transformations in the domain of workers' security, understood as the perspective of stable employment with the same employer during the bulk of one's occupational career. Nowadays, the meaning of the term security evolves towards a new paradigm. According to that paradigm, work has become more 'flexible' and the workers need to acquire the skill of adapting to frequent changes in the labour market. This often means the necessity of retraining, improving competence and being open to the perspective of professional and spatial mobility (Kalina-Prasznic, 2009; Marx, 2014). At the same time, this leads to the situation in which a great number of workers experience uncertainty as to whether or not they will find new employment quickly following a potential loss of their current job (Standing, 2011). As Green (2009, p. 344) argues:

these changes imply that workers are required to take on greater shares of individual risk and to expect less job security than hitherto.

Furthermore, Glavin (2013, p. 119) notes the social and economic consequences carried by that change:

Finally, the absence of secure, long-term employment may reduce individual's tendency to engage in certain actions that require long-term planning, such as starting a family or purchasing a home - behaviours that may otherwise foster positive beliefs about personal control.

In an increasing number of cases, having an open-ended job based on an employment contract does not itself guarantee the accomplishment of personal and collective (most usually household-level) goals. In particular, those earning minimum wage are forced to undertake additional, casual work in order to reach a satisfactory level of income security. The essence of being an employee has changed as well and it currently encompasses new, flexible forms of employment. All these changes have been succinctly summarised by Edgell (2006, p. 12):

> *Thus employment is no longer a simple matter of being in or out of work, employed or unemployed, but more the matter of degree characterized by an employment continuum that ranges from zero employment to over-employment.*

It should be noted, however, that the above-mentioned changes have not affected all categories of employees to the same extent. A noticeable division has emerged within the working population, the main dimensions of it being the form of employment and, indirectly, access (or a lack thereof) to welfare benefits. Labour markets have been subject to a split into at least two segments (Bauder, 2006). Those employed within first of them are mostly highly qualified professionals, enjoying a much higher level of labour market security than those employed within the second one. More often than not, migrants end up in the latter, less attractive segment. This polarisation is well defined by the concept of 'good' and 'bad' jobs, put forward by Kalleberg (2011). Focusing on the case of the United States, that author observed that permanent employment had never been such a socially diversifying attribute as it is in modern societies. As Boeri and van Ours (2008) point out, workers employed on contracts for an indefinite period of time, especially in the first segment populated by highly qualified employees, can still count on higher level of legal protection of their employment. But the rapidly growing number of workers employed for a fixed-term, the self-employed and those employed on the so-called zero-hours contracts cannot. At the same time, the profound changes to labour markets, which can be observed in virtually all advanced industrial societies, lead to the widening of the division between those enjoying the stability of employment — thanks to, among others, active labour market policies and the presence of trade unions — and the growing population of those deprived of access to the institutions of employment protection. This distinction is especially pronounced in the case of immigrants. They are highly overrepresented among those employed under the conditions of uncertainty, being rarely covered by a system of protection and having restricted access to welfare benefits. In their case, gaining labour market security tends to be much more difficult than it is for native workers.

In the context of the debates on the evolution of human labour, terms such as 'precariat' and the 'precarians' are often used by scholars, journalists and politicians. The concept and the notion of the 'precariat' are useful in describing recent changes taking place in the world of labour. The term denotes a growing category, or class, of people working and living under the ('precarious') conditions of permanent uncertainty and insecurity, resulting from their inferior and underprivileged labour market status (Standing, 2011). Obviously, migrants, as a category, are at high risk of becoming precarians. Standing (2002, p. 442) has pointed to the following seven work-related dimensions of security, typical of the industrial era (Fordism):

(1) *labour market security — adequate employment and work opportunities, through high levels of employment ensured by macroeconomic policy;*

(2) *employment security — protection against arbitrary dismissal, and employment stability compatible with economic dynamism;*

(3) *job security* — *a post linked to an occupation or 'career', plus tolerance of demarcation practices, barriers to skill dilution, craft boundaries, job qualifications, etc.;*

(4) *work security* — *protection against accidents and illness at work, through safety and health regulations, limits on working time, on unsociable hours, and on night work for women, etc.;*

(5) *skill reproduction security* — *widespread opportunities to gain and retain skills, through apprenticeships, vocational training, etc.;*

(6) *income security* — *protection of income through minimum wage machinery, wage indexation, comprehensive social security, progressive taxation, etc.;*

(7) *representation security* — *protection of collective voice in the labour market, through independent trade unions and employers; associations and other bodies able to represent the interests of workers and working communities.*

Standing (2011) argues that today's employees are being successively denied the aforementioned privileges, which limits the possibility of gaining labour market security. This sort of a sharp statement seems to be too pessimistic and too general, however. We should rather speak about changing meanings of particular aspects of security and their relations to the character, time and place of performing work. The aforementioned types of security will thus be evaluated and sought with varying intensities depending on the particular category of workers, their qualifications and work experience. The accomplishment of just one of the types of security mentioned by Standing can have an impact on the general feeling of stability in the labour market and thus lead to the right' state of income security. This, in turn, would translate into social and economic security. For example, a person with a high level of job security can have a much lower level of employment security and vice versa. For some workers, especially the less qualified ones, it will be more important to gain a satisfactory level of income security at the cost of skill reproduction security or representation security. We should also be aware that nowadays we are witnessing a very critical change; that is, many countries are moving away from the model based on job security towards one emphasising employment security. Auer (2010, p. 381) emphasises some even further-reaching changes:

> *The decisive and critical shift is thus not from job security to employment security, but towards what can be called labour market security. Labour market security implies that security for workers in today's labour markets cannot stem from job and employment security alone. It has to be complemented by additional layers of security.*

From the point of view of this study, special attention is paid to three essential categories of security, which seem to be crucial from the perspective of migrant workers: income security, employment security and job security. While the desire to reach a high level of income security is characteristic of the vast majority of workers, the situation appears to be far more nuanced in the cases of job and employment security. Some workers can choose job security as the desirable model of obtaining income security, that is, security on the labour market. Others display greater risk acceptance, preferring a model based on employment security. It indeed seems that, in spite of all the structural changes in the labour market, from the viewpoint of a large part of the working population, job security is still an important and desirable element of labour relations. It can have greater subjective importance than pay, benefits, job-skills training or career development opportunities (Probst & Jiang, 2017). At the same time, a growing proportion of workers are aware of the often inevitable necessity of responding and adapting to new conditions of employment, created by the demand side of labour relations. More often than not, a situation in which one does not experience overwhelming difficulties when searching for a job, that is, employment security, is a combination of flexible and stable jobs. It is worth paying attention to the ways of defining these two kinds of security, to determinants of their high or low level, as well as to the approaches to measurement applied in relevant comparative research.

JOB SECURITY AND EMPLOYMENT SECURITY

In spite of the aforementioned structural changes to labour markets, job security continues to be an important element of labour relations. Scholars argue that, alongside autonomy, it is a constitutive component of the quality of work and employment (Gallie, 2017). The extant scholarly literature on job security analyses it from a number of perspectives, including the psychological, the economic and the legal one. Research on the impact of job security or insecurity on the behaviour of workers dates back to the 1980s. The most general definition maintains that job security refers to the situation in which one retains the same job with the same employer for a long time (Muffels, Crouch, & Wilthagen, 2014, p. 101). In accordance with this interpretation, an emphasis is put on the stability of employment in one place for as long as possible. Other authors focus on analysing job insecurity, defined in terms of a threat of unemployment (De Witte, 2005) or, more broadly, as an 'anticipated involuntary job loss' (Greenhalgh & Rosenblatt, 2010). Existing literature on the topic also points out that job security has an irreducible subjective component. It is emphasised that individual workers would differ in their assessment as regards the extent to which they have accomplished labour market security through job security. For example, Näswall and De Witte (2003) observe that, depending on personality traits, age and family situation, two persons working under the exact same employment conditions may display radically different self-perceived levels of job-related security.

In addition, scholars have been looking for general regularities as regards the perceptions of the essence of job security and differences in its evaluations between particular categories of workers (Kiersztyn, 2018; Kinnunen, Mauno, Nätti, & Happonen, 1999; Mohr, 2000; Näswall & De Witte, 2003). The following general relationships can be distinguished based on such perceptions and evaluations:

- Older employees (over 50 years of age) are more prone to value job security than are the younger ones, as a result of, among other things, the fear that they would not find their way on the labour market in case they lose their present employment.

- Men are more likely than women to experience stress resulting from the fear of losing a job, which means a higher level of self-perceived job insecurity. This is perhaps due to the fact that men's labour is still the main source of income for many households.

- More often than not, labour market security in the public sector is based on job security, which is a major factor reducing the aggregate level of job insecurity. At the same time, the highest levels of job insecurity are faced by those employed by small private firms.

- The youngest cohorts of employees, often aware of the changes on labour market, tend to accept worse conditions of employment. They may actually be less interested in job security because of the relative lack of financial burdens or family obligations. In contrast, it may also be related to these people's limited experience in the labour market.

- Blue-collar and low-skilled workers are at a higher risk of losing a job, and this is the cause of a high level of anxiety concerning their present employment, their position on the labour market and the uncertainty as regards the events that would follow a potential loss of a job. Thus, they strive for job security.

The term and the concept of employment security had gained in popularity at the turn of the twentieth and twenty-first centuries, following the quick rise of the so-called flexible forms of employment. It was a response to rapid changes in the labour markets of highly developed countries. It was also related to the European Commission's official stance on the 'ideal' model of labour markets, based on the so-called flexicurity (European Commission, 2007). The approach promoted by the Commission involves combining flexible forms of employment and thus the possibility of frequent job switching, with an extensive system of state-funded protection for the temporarily unemployed as well as advanced systems of retraining and job placement services. In this context, regulating the economy in such a way as to stimulate the demand for labour on part of the employers is of key importance as well. From the perspective of workers, this would increase the chances of finding a new job easily and relatively quickly. The implications of this idea include the above-mentioned employment security as well as the promotion of the concept of employability, that is, providing opportunities for a relatively quick re-employment following a job loss. Pruijt and Derogee (2010, p. 439) argue that nowadays we are witnessing 'the death of job security' and note that 'enhanced employability is the new job security'. While job security, as depicted earlier, refers to maintaining work with the same employer, employment security is based on the ability to have frequent changes of employment unaccompanied by a deterioration of conditions of work and pay (Muffels & Wilthagen, 2013). The key element in this context is the chance of re-employment, that is, employability, which, as Marx (2014, p. 353) notes, should reduce job insecurities. The essence of that kind of work-related security is succinctly explained in the following passage from the work by Muffels and Wilthagen (2013, p. 114):

In the 'new' employment relationship the job security offered through life-time employment and the international labour market is substituted by employment security offered through investments in the employability of employees by provisions for training and learning opportunities which raise the general skill-level.

Similar to job security, employment security does also have a subjective component. This means that self-perceptions of employment security will differ between individuals and across particular employment situations. This subjective dimension is usually measured relying on survey items which require the interviewees to rate the degree of their fear of losing a job and chances of finding a new one. The review of the survey instruments designed to extract the perceptions of job and employment security[1] applied in international comparative research programmes, such as the European Working Conditions Survey, the European Social Survey and the Eurobarometer, suggests that they are highly incongruous with respect to time perspective in which the worker anticipates a change, or a lack thereof, in her current employment situation. The perceptions of job and employment security are measured in the time horizon of six months, 24 months or, sometimes, with no exactly specified time perspective. A summary of the review of those measures is presented in **Table 1**.

In spite of the relative irreducibility of the subjective dimension of job and employment security, there obviously exists a large catalogue of objective determinants of the levels of labour market security. Workers' self-perceived prospective evaluations of their own fortunes as the outcomes of the functioning of labour markets are affected by a number of micro-, meso- and macro-factors. As the aforementioned discussion suggests, it is the personal situation of each worker that has a substantial impact on the subjective importance she would attach to particular dimensions of labour market security. For example, educational attainment or access to social networks reducing the feeling of uncertainty on the labour market is of vital importance. On the other hand, a number of studies have demonstrated that macro-level factors, especially unemployment rates, may have effect on the levels of stress suffered by those searching for a job (De Cuyper, Bernhard-Oettel, Berntson, De Witte, & Alarco, 2008). The presence and effective functioning of various associations dealing with the issues of labour protection, mainly trade unions, also affects the conditions of employment, especially for the workers characterised by a strong fear of losing their jobs (see Kiersztyn, 2018). The existing legal provisions, especially the guarantees concerning protection of employment and the rights of laid-off employees, codetermine the level of job or employment security as well. The awareness of the possibility

Table 1. Summary of Measurement Instruments for Job Security and Employment Security in Major International Social Survey Programmes.

	European Working Conditions Survey (EWCS) 2015	European Social Survey (ESS) 2010	Eurobarometer (European Commission, 2011)
Job security	• I might lose my job in the next six months	• My job is secure	• How confident would you say you are in your ability to keep your job in the coming months (very, fairly, not very)? • Would you say that you are very confident, fairly confident, not very confident, or not at all confident in having a job in two years' time?
Employment security	• If I were to lose or quit my current job, it would be easy for me to find a job of a similar salary	• How difficult or easy would it be for you to get a similar or better job with another employer if you had to leave your current job?	• Combination of job security and labour market security (i.e. If you were to be laid-off, how would you rate on a scale of 1–10, the likelihood of you finding a job in the next six months?

Source: Authors' own elaboration based on European Commission (2011), ESS Round 5: European Social Survey Round 5 Data (2010), and Eurofound (2019).

of taking advantage of the common state-funded benefits, especially those for the unemployed and earning below the minimum wage, is yet another kind of 'safety valve' for employees. As a result of a review of the existing literature on the topic, we put forward a classification of the factors affecting workers' subjective perceptions of job and employment security. We group those factors into the following four dimensions: human and social capital indicators, macro-level economic parameters, formal institutions and, finally, the country-level model of labour relations and employment policy (see Table 2).

Undoubtedly, the issues discussed earlier may have far-reaching consequences for our understanding of international migration processes. A question thus arises as to whether or not migrants' individual decisions, contributing to the shape of the aforementioned processes, are affected by job and employment security considerations. More precisely, it seems worth asking if the factors enumerated in Table 2, especially the macro-level ones, have an impact on migration-related decisions, such as the choice of a destination of migration. In the next section, we thus take a closer look at the aforementioned factors in the context of labour migration. We attempt to distinguish those of them that may play a vital role in shaping the decisions of migrants, especially from the viewpoint of labour market security as one of the desired outcomes of an individual migration project.

LABOUR MARKET SECURITY AS A CO-DETERMINANT OF MIGRATION DECISIONS

As Castles, de Haas, and Miller (2014, pp. 25–27) note, a decision to leave one's place of residence and work, especially a decision to leave one's native country, is an outcome of

Table 2. Factors Affecting Job and Employment Security.

Human and Social Capital Indicators	Macro-level Economic Parameters	Formal Institutions	Country-level Model of Labour Relations and Employment Policy
• level of education • professional experience • personal traits (e.g. Inclination to take risks) • family situation • quality and scope of social networks	• level of unemployment (including long-term unemployment) • the number of vacancies • average level of remuneration • obligatory minimum wages • level of social expenditures	• level of unionisation and power of trade unions • activity of work standards and safety inspectorate • activity of NGOs • functional quality of labour market institutions (e.g. employment agencies, job centres)	• types of contracts and their scope • employment Protection Legislation • collective bargaining in force • access to benefits for the unemployed • life-long learning • vocational training • active labour market policy

Source: Authors' own proposal based on the works by Dixon, Fullerton, and Robertson (2013), Kiersztyn (2018).

complex process. It is influenced by numerous factors, often interacting with one another. As such, it appears to be a resultant of a co-occurrence of a multitude of predictors, including social, economic, political as well as cultural ones (Kaczmarczyk & Kloc-Nowak, 2018).

Our review of migration theories points to a universal pattern, according to which migration is generally an important strategy in the life of an individual. People's decisions to emigrate voluntarily thus tend to be based on rational premises. Voluntary migration, be it labour or educational migration, may also bring tangible benefits to both the emigrating individuals and the community sending them out. It seems to be generally expected that emigration would lead to the accomplishment of the desired conditions of living and employment, superior to those offered by one's country of origin (Kubitsky, 2012). A calculus of the pros and cons of emigration is a substantial element of the process of planning and then making decisions concerning spatial mobility. Assuming fairly unrestricted access to relevant information, a person considering migration can make meaningful comparisons between her country of origin and the prospective country of destination. Scholars nonetheless emphasise the lack of a consistent catalogue of causes which would allow an explanation of why only a part of a population decide to adopt the migration strategy within the period of their economic activity[2] (Brettell & Hollifield, 2015). At the same time, it is argued that, for instance, migration decisions of a highly qualified professional will be driven by radically different motives than those of an unskilled seasonal worker, while the motivation of a refugee fleeing from a territory of an armed conflict or a natural disaster will again have its own peculiarities (see Castles et al., 2014; Kaczmarczyk & Kloc-Nowak, 2018).

At the micro-level, socio-demographic traits of individuals and households may affect the propensity for considering migration as a viable life strategy. In particular, a focus on households is a distinctive characteristic of the theory of new economy of migration (Stark, 1991). According to that concept, individuals' decisions, even if seen as autonomous, cannot be interpreted in complete separation from the views of her household members and even the members of the broader community that she comes from. In this context, the approach emphasising 'family portfolio diversification decisions', whereby migration abroad of a family member serves to hedge against risky labour markets in the home country, is of particular interest (Bodvarsson & Van den Berg, 2009, p. 53).

The status of the predominant theoretical perspective, helping us understand why people decide to migrate, should perhaps be reserved for the push-pull model. As Kaczmarczyk (2005, p. 29) noted, the concept was a ground-breaking one at the time of its beginnings and still is among the most influential ones in the area of studies of migrations. Its original proponent, Lee (1966), distinguished four groups of factors taken into consideration while migration-related decisions are made:

(1) push factors characterising the place of origin;

(2) pull factors characterising the place of destination;

(3) intervening obstacles; and

(4) personal factors.

According to the push-pull model, a migration-related decision is taken on the basis of a crucial disparity between the two localisations. In this context, 'push and pull factors' interact with each an individual's resource pool, needs and experiences. The decision to migrate is a complex compromise between the incentives to go, the capacity to go, and the perceived costs and benefits (Krasteva, McDonnell, & Tolgensbakk, 2019, p. 162). The exact factors taken into consideration while making a decision to migrate are obviously seen through the lens of one's subjectivity. The interpretation of such factors depends on a number of personal traits, such as education, experience on the labour market or age, to mention just a few. Lee (1966) assumed that migrating individuals had in their minds a certain prior 'image' of the country of destination. And yet, the prospective evaluation of the future localisation is hindered by the fact that the information available is usually incomplete and thus at least partially inadequate. This may cause decisions viewed retrospectively as erroneous, be it with respect to the binary choice between migration and staying home or regarding the choice of the country of destination. However, because one's knowledge of the country of origin is certainly more profound than that of a country of destination, the strength of the 'pull' factors must be quite pronounced if the decision to migrate is to be made (Kaczmarczyk, 2005).

From the very moment of publication of Lee's work (1966), scholars criticised the push-pull model as too simplistic and deterministic (de Haas, 2011; Skeldon, 1997). Among others, Lee's opponents pointed to the static character of the theory. At the same time, they emphasise that the decision to migrate is a very complex process, undergoing numerous modifications, depending on circumstances and the changes of the migrants' motivations (de Haas, 2011). Skeldon (1997) argues that push-pull theories focus mainly on pecuniary and environmental considerations. In spite of the criticism, a number of authors, trying to develop new theoretical conceptualisations explaining the motives of migration, pay special attention to comparisons of the country of origin with the potential country of destination (see Baláž & Williams, 2018). Some of them, for instance, point out the pattern according to which push factors play a more important role in the case of unskilled migrants, while pull factors are more important for migrants with higher qualifications (Kazlauskienė & Rinkevičius, 2006). At the same time, however, it should be acknowledged that the technological progress, with ensuing broadening of access to information and to instruments of its verification, for example through social media, throws a new light on the strengths and weaknesses of push and pull theory. Using the Internet, a today's potential migrant can obtain much more knowledge than a migrant few years ago. Some criticisms of the push and pull theory, especially those questioning its plausibility, have thus lost much of their validity. It seems to open an avenue for a revival of the concept.

Notwithstanding the discussion about the relative significance of the particular drivers of the process of making migration-related decisions, the disparities in earnings seem to be the most important of those factors (Castles et al., 2014). Nonetheless, limiting the set of predictors of the decisions to migrate to differences in wages only would be an over-simplification. A growing number of scholars look for and analyse other factors affecting the decisions to migrate as well as the choice of the country of destination. It appears that the conditions of employment and the possibility of self-realisation in the country of destination are also important (Kazlauskienė & Rinkevičius, 2006). It seems that the issue of labour market security is not trivial either and that, depending on a migrants' preferences, the choice of the country of destination can be co-determined by the model of labour market security, predominant in a particular country (job security vs employment security).

The issue of labour market security is one of the themes which appear in the studies analysing the expectations of migrants, albeit its relationships with job security and employment security have not thus far been explicitly explored. For example, for lower-educated immigrants, job security means predominantly a permanent contract and 'decent work' (Kremer, 2016). Such notions as broadly conceived security, stability, safety or peace are considered highly significant and desirable while making decisions to migrate (see Grzymała-Kazłowska, 2018, p. 257). The experience of job insecurity is the factor pushing migrants from their country of origin. Emigration is expected to improve their situation and bring about an improvement in their living conditions (Krasteva et al., 2019). For instance, in the course of research carried out among Polish immigrants after Poland's accession to EU it turned out 20% of the interviewed respondents indicated that the lack of hope of finding a job in Poland had been a factor stimulating their decisions to emigrate (Strzelecki, Saczuk, Grabowska, & Kotowska, 2015, p. 148). This observation is echoed by other studies on the determinants of emigration from Poland (see Szczygielska, 2013). Notably, one's failing to accomplish a satisfactory level of labour market security in the country of destination is sometimes pointed to as a potential motive for return migration (see Friberg, 2012). Overall, the aforementioned studies seem to suggest that the issue of labour market security can be both a push and a pull factor. It is a push factor because the potential migrant faces a choice between putting up with the state of suspension and uncertainty regarding the fulfilment of her and her household's needs and aspirations and a decision to emigrate to another country in order to attain income security. However, labour market security may be thought of as a pull factor, especially in the context of immigration and labour market policies implemented in a country of destination. If such policies are designed to attract labour force from abroad, migrants coming to a particular labour market will possibly be able to get employment and income making them feel secure. Essentially, a migration-receiving state faces a choice between two models. It can implement a model based on either job security or employment security. The choice will have a significant effect on both the socio-economic profiles of immigrants and the length of their period of residence. Furthermore, policy shifts constraining the scope of labour market security enjoyed by foreigners may result in their return to the country of origin or a departure to another migration-receiving country. To reiterate what was already said above, the key issue from the viewpoint of labour market security is gaining income security through either job security or employment security. In the light of this, migrants choose countries where they can get possibly high and satisfactory pay for their work.

Securing for themselves a relatively high and regular income from the very beginning of their stay in a receiving country tends to be a priority for labour migrants. Numbers of studies demonstrate that the so-called short-term or seasonal workers, often migrating in order to earn money covering the cost of a one-off goal, are guided by the desire of achieving a high level of income security (see Iglicka & Gmaj, 2013; Vollmer, 2016). Short-term-oriented newcomers are usually interested in finding employment fast, preferably immediately, even at the cost of putting up with worse conditions of employment (Kogan, 2007). They thus attach less weight to working time or issues such as occupational health and safety. The core and dominant element of their migration strategy is the accumulation of financial capital and thereby the satisfaction of a clearly identifiable need. For instance, a study by Parutis (2014), conducted among migrants from East European countries in the United Kingdom, demonstrated that, at the beginning of their stay in the United Kingdom, it is a deliberate use of the services provided by job agencies that constitutes the chief possibility of securing a relatively stable income relatively quickly. If an agency offers another better-paid job they most often accept such an offer and switch employers. Their strategy is thus that of employment security. Only when they gain experience and accumulate some money do they start to strive for the stability of employment. Most usually, this means more secure employment as well as the acquisition of workers' rights. They thus largely switch strategies from employment security to job security. This also reduces the burden of transactional costs, such as fees paid to employment agencies. In this context, it is also important to have a relative economic security, that is, accumulated savings. As Friberg (2012, pp. 1599–1601) observes, having spare financial resources is an important precondition of effective long-term planning. It also facilitates making autonomous decisions, including decisions to switch employers.

In the context of migrations both within and to the EU, it is worth noting that income security is a particularly desirable element of labour relations for immigrants from third countries, that is, those not being members of the EU or the European Economic Area, coming to the EU member states. Due to the immigration regulations in force in the EU member states, those workers usually have restricted access to better job offers. They thus tend to undertake employment within the so-called second segment of the respective labour market (Piore, 1979). As a result, the pursuit for stable, monthly pay is a fundamental element in their migration strategies. Unlike many workers coming from within the EU, third-country labour migrants thus suffer from permanent anxiety of being taken advantage of by fraudulent employers, deliberately failing to pay them the agreed wage. Research carried out among Ukrainians pursuing employment both in Poland and in other EU member states largely corroborates the above intuition (Kindler, 2011; Xypolytas, 2017). Nonetheless, while facing a likely violation of workers' rights, Ukrainian immigrants usually decide to remain in Poland. In their home country, the pay for the jobs that are available to them is simply too low to be a source of any security. The nearly everlasting economic recession, affecting the Ukrainian economy for years, has been taking its toll in the domain of labour relations, with the delays in wage paying reaching several months (Kindler, 2011). We thus clearly observe a classic example of push and pull factors in action in this case. As Vollmer (2016) notes, Ukrainians often conceive of employment abroad as a chance of accumulating resources enabling them to pay off liabilities (mostly credits) and thereby stabilise their financial situation. Thus, even the rather uncomfortable situation in the receiving country, a situation marked by uncertainty of getting paid, is still better in their view than is the permanent disillusionment in this respect in their home country. Iglicka and Gmaj (2013) note that the decisions of Ukrainian nationals are often taken in the context of a household and that the money transfers are a key factor sustaining the circular migrations between Poland and Ukraine. It can therefore be assumed that a potential increase in income security in Ukraine could stimulate return migration. However, in case of a lack of improvement in the native country, accompanied by an increase in the scale of fraud in the primary receiving country and the associated reduction of income security, could generate incentives for searching for new destinations of migration.

LABOUR MARKET SECURITY FROM THE PERSPECTIVE OF ACHIEVEMENT OF MIGRATION GOALS

'Normal Life'

One of the motives, appearing quite often in labour migrants' autobiographical narratives, is the prospects of the so-called normal life. Regardless of the country of destination, migrants compare their situation in the receiving country to that of the sending one, evaluating the conditions of both broadly conceived life and employment. It turns out that not only is the pursuit for a 'better life' a factor behind emigration, but it can also effectively prevent returning to the country of origin. For instance, in her study of the situation of Polish immigrants' families in Norway, Ślusarczyk (2019) observed that their main reason for emigration from Poland was the urge to 'run away' from the necessity of 'ceaseless work' and disappointing conditions of employment. This suggests that labour market security is being perceived by migrants as one of the core elements of their concept of a 'normal life'. In addition, Ślusarczyk (2019) emphasises that the migrants she studied viewed work in Poland as low-quality and offering income below the level guaranteeing self-sufficiency and the ability of effective planning of one's future. Again, we are dealing with efforts to enhance one's labour market security and thereby improve the quality, broadly conceived, of one's life.

Finding oneself in the situation of 'living normal life' is an important precondition of economic integration of immigrants in the receiving country. The notion of 'normalcy' appears repeatedly in autobiographical narratives of post-accession labour migrants. Terms such as 'decent life', 'peaceful life', 'decent working life', or 'living with dignity' are often used to explain the advantages of being a migrant (Bygnes & Erdal, 2017; Galasińska & Kozłowska, 2009; White, 2017). Bygnes and Erdal (2017, p. 110) point out that in migrants' views 'normal life' is associated with general security, a dimension of it being a 'certain degree of predictability about future earnings'. In the opinion of migrants working in the United Kingdom, 'normal life' means also the right of access to welfare benefits for families and state-funded health services. In the case of female workers, the arrangements facilitating their return to the labour market following maternity leave seem to play a critical role as well (Drinkwater & Garapich, 2015). When all the aforementioned conditions are met, labour market security can exert an extremely positive impact on the life of migrants and their families, especially in the context of procreation plans (e.g. Creese, Dyck, & McLaren, 2008).

The accomplishment of the self-perceived state of 'normalcy' and 'living decent life' is feasible for both those with a preference for job security and those that value employment security. Job security, under the conditions of a satisfactory pay and the ability of returning to work following maternity or paternity leave, seems to be an optimal situation. In contrast, the state of 'normal life' can also be reached by those pursuing 'flexible security' (employment security). The situation of labour migrants in the United Kingdom is a clear example of this. The constitutive characteristics of the British labour market, especially the relative prevalence of self-employment, short-term jobs or zero-hour contracts, create the possibility of adapting the place of work to the particular worker's situation. For example, young people, especially those with no family burden, may agree to work longer hours, exceeding the regular workload. In this way, they can relatively quickly save larger sums of money for specific purposes, such as prolonged travelling abroad. As Grzymała-Kazłowska (2018, p. 206) argues, although undoubtedly 'flexible', the British labour market is indeed perceived as secure by the vast majority of labour migrants. This is largely echoed by the conclusions reached by Cieslik (2011) in the course of her research on Poles working in the United Kingdom. Her interviewees tended to indicate that they viewed their employment within the 'flexible' British labour market as more stable and secure than their past work in Poland. At the same time, they feel far less exploited and look into the future with much more confidence. For young highly qualified employees, that is, for the ones particularly attractive for employers, there is a choice between stable contracts and taking advantage of 'flexible solutions'. Again, a fairly comfortable state of labour market security can be reached through either job security or employment security. Additional advantages of 'flexible' forms of employment, such as the opportunity of combining child care with part-time work, seem to be evident as well (Parutis, 2014).

Welfare Magnet

Welfare systems constitute another factor affecting migration-related decisions. Extensive welfare state institutions may contribute to the comfort of migrants' functioning in the receiving country, regardless of whether the predominant labour market model emphasises job security or employment security. Migrants are aware that countries implementing generous systems of benefits can be attractive for them, especially at times of unemployment or occupational passivity caused by maternal obligations. The benefits reduce the risk of a loss of a 'normal life', resulting from such temporary interruptions in one's work career. This applies especially to migrants perceiving labour market security in terms of job security and thus being reluctant to accept frequent job switching. It is the access to benefits for the unemployed and for families with children that bears particular significance as a determinant of their feeling of security. Extensive systems of benefits can nonetheless be advantageous also for those following the model of employment security. During periods of transition from one job to another, state-funded benefits can help them minimise the temporary decrease in income, thus freeing them from the necessity of undertaking a suboptimal job. Such an approach to the role of various benefits is explicitly practiced in countries implementing the so-called flexicurity model, especially in Denmark (Madsen, 1999).

Since the 1980s, scholars have sought to answer the question about the extent to which generosity and accessibility of the welfare state influence migration strategies (Gaston & Rajaguru, 2013). It is generally assumed that the cross-country differences in social transfers and social services constitute a predictor of migration flows, provided that immigrants are entitled to participate in a wide range of public support schemes. In the course of his study of the impact of welfare systems on the patterns of international migrations, Borjas (1999) put forward the so-called welfare magnet hypothesis. According to his concept, welfare generosity of rich countries constitutes a crucial pull factor as immigrants choose the countries where they can gain access to an extensive range of social benefits. Such a strategy protects them from potential labour market risks. However, as Razin and Wahba (2011) note, the applicability of the 'welfare magnet hypothesis' is rather limited. Its explanatory potential seems to be confined to the cases of free-migration regimes, the best example being migrations within the borders of the EU. It also turns out that the welfare magnet has a greater impact on the behaviour of low-skilled workers, that is, the main net beneficiaries of the system of social benefits (Razin & Wahba, 2011). High-skilled immigrants tend to actually choose countries with lower social expenditures and, at the same time, lower taxes. It is thus perhaps a relatively small tax burden rather than welfare systems that constitutes a factor attracting highly qualified foreign professionals (Brücker et al., 2002).

Employment Protection and the Role of Official Institutions

Employment protection legislation and the efficiency of the state institutions responsible for its implementation constitute yet another set of factors playing an important role in determining the levels of labour market security offered to immigrants. Although some would certainly classify those aspects as belonging to the area of welfare, they nonetheless form a more general dimension of guarantees of labour market security (see Mai, 2019). It is worth emphasising that the legal status of a given immigrant (EU citizen versus third-country citizen) implies the scope of access to particular public/state institutions dealing with, among other things, the protection of workers' rights. In the case of free movement of persons within the EU, such access is entirely unrestricted, while for third-country citizens many restrictions apply. However, some support with regard to issues related to the broadly conceived functioning on labour markets in the receiving countries can be obtained from immigrant associations (NGOs), established as a result of the increased influx of foreigners (Nowosielski, 2011).

Extant literature on the topic puts a special emphasis on the role of employment protection and its impact on both the scale and the directions of migration. Paradoxically, as demonstrated by Cigagna and Sulis (2015), increasing labour market security through raising job security tends to reduce the influx of new immigrants to a respective country. This is almost certainly because their access to job offers is severely restricted. In addition, employers may display more trust in native workers and thus have a strong preference for hiring them rather than immigrants. After all, hiring a foreigner and facing the obligation of nearly instant stabilisation of her position is a fairly risky step. However, foreigners residing permanently in a receiving country are covered by labour protection legislation to the same extent as is applied to native workers. Accordingly, Geis, Uebelmesser and Werding (2013) have demonstrated that labour market security, conceived of in terms of advanced legislation protecting workers' rights and a strong position of trade unions, plays a more important role in lives of the permanent settlers in receiving countries than in those of short-term labour immigrants. Also, Bazillier and Moullan (2012) note that employment protection legislation may make the passage from unemployment to employment slower for foreigners than for native workers. It would have far-reaching consequences for the composition of the population of immigrants; short-term migrants will be discouraged to come and stay, while those with longer-term migration plans will be ready to overcome the initial obstacles.

It also seems that an important variable, especially in countries such as the United Kingdom or Germany, is the citizenship of the migrants. As Kogan (2007, p. 289) notes:

Indeed, stricter employment-protection legislation seems to be responsible for the larger employment disadvantages of recent third-country immigrants.

In other words, we can say that countries preferring models based on job security and thus implementing advanced systems of employment protection tend to be less open to the influx of new immigrants than are states with more flexible forms of employment in place.

Furthermore, it turns out that the broadly conceived transparency of particular labour market institutions, such as employment agencies and offices for foreigners, is of equally great importance for third-country immigrants. For example, Vollmer's (2016) recent research, carried out among immigrants from Ukraine, pointed to the fact that in their autobiographical narratives they tended to compare the institutional dimension in Ukraine to that in the receiving country. The high level of corruption, affecting labour relations just as the entire economic sphere, is a yet another factor discouraging many Ukrainians to stay in their home country. At the same time, Ukrainians value legal order and well-organised public institutions that guarantee protection to workers in the receiving countries. Andrejuk (2017) reaches similar conclusions, pointing out that Ukrainians living and working in Poland rate the quality of public institutions in the receiving country as much higher than for their counterparts in Ukraine. The opposite is true in the case of Spaniards and Britons working in Poland who are generally critical of Polish public institutions. We can therefore safely assume that the efficiency of institutions, especially those offering retraining or opportunities for raising qualifications, may affect the well-being of immigrants, especially those that prefer employment security and are thus interested in making use of such services at times of transition between employers.

Finally, a strong position of trade unions and other organisations acting for the rights of workers, including foreign ones, is also indicated as an important element in the context of labour market security (Kiersztyn, 2018). One example is the case of immigrants in Denmark, experiencing a high level of flexibility in the labour market. They, however, note the presence of unemployment insurance and the assistance of trade unions as factors mitigating the unwanted consequences of this particular setup of labour relations (Pljevaljcic-Simkunas & Thomsen, 2018).

SUMMARY – THE MODEL OF SECURITY IN THE STUDY OF LABOUR MIGRATIONS

The intensification of deep changes taking place in labour markets since the beginning of the twenty-first century, and the associated transformation of labour relations, affect the functioning of workers and the society as a whole. One of the most recognisable dimensions of this process is the loss of predictability as regards employment and a deficit of work-related security. The shrinkage of security on labour market inevitably brings harm to income security. In principle, security can still be accomplished by means of adaptation and adjustment to the occurring changes. This, however, requires a permanent effort directed at the enhancement of competences. Intense migration flows should be added to this picture. For a significant and still growing category of workers, achieving income security is possible through migration, that is, searching for a country where the knowledge, skills and experience of a particular worker will be put to good use and remunerated more generously than in the country of origin. The desire for a better pay is both a push and a pull factor. At the same time, income security can be accomplished in a number of different ways. In the present work, we have analysed issues related to job and employment security, that is, two distinct models of pursuing labour market security, preferred by two distinct categories of persons (migrants). We argue that the application of this perspective to explaining migration-related decisions contributes to a better understanding of why some individuals decided to migrate while others did not and why a particular category of migrants chose a given country of destination. It allows for filling in some gaps in the existing knowledge about the complexity of migration decisions. Reaching the state of income security through either job security or employment security is directly associated with the notion of 'normal life', that is, a satisfactory standard of living and the ability to accomplish the main life purposes of an individual or her respective household. This is particularly demonstrable in the case of migrants from Central and Eastern Europe (CEE) countries, facing the micro-level consequences of structural problems on labour market in their native countries. The review of the extant literature suggests that there are crucial differences in perceiving worker security between the EU citizens taking advantage of the free flow of workers and third-country immigrants. A disparity exists with respect to both labour market security in the narrower sense, including protection of workers' fundamental rights and the broader social security affected by various social benefits and the institutions of social policy. Last but not least, the choice between models emphasising either job security or employment security in order to accomplish income security seems to also depend on factors such as an immigrant's level of education, her confidence of functioning on the labour market as well as the planned period of stay in the host country.

NOTES

1. More often than not, the analyses in question aim to extract the degree of job insecurity.

2. According to the data of IOM, in 2015, there were 244 million international migrants, which made up only 3% of the population of the world.

REFERENCES

Andrejuk, K. (2017). Znaczenie polskiej sfery welfare dla imigrantów. Opinie i praktyki ludności napływowej z wybranych krajów europejskich. *Studia BAS*, 2(50), 107–128.

Auer, P. (2010). What's in a name? The rise (and fall?) of flexicurity. *Journal of Industrial Relations*, 52(3), 371–386. doi:10.1177/0022185610365646

Baláž, V., & Williams, A. M. (2018). Migration decision in the face of upheaval: An experimental approach. *Population, Space and Place*, 24(1), 2115–2127. doi:10.1002/psp.2115

Bauder, H. (2006). *Labour movement. How migration regulates labour markets?* Oxford: Oxford University Press.

Bazillier, R., & Moullan, Y. (2012). *Employment protection and migration.* Retrieved from http://remi.bazillier.free.fr/bazillier_moullan_dec2012.pdf

Bodvarsson, Ö. B., & Ven den Berg, H. (2009). *The economics of immigration: Theory and policy.* Heidelberg: Springer.

Boeri, T., & van Ours, J. (2008). *The economics of imperfect labor markets.* Princeton, NJ: Princeton University Press.

Borjas, G. J. (1999). Immigration and welfare magnets. *Journal of Labor Economics*, 17(4), 607–637.

Brettell, C. B., & Hollifield, J. F. (2015). The sociology of international migration. In C. B. Brettell & J. F. Hollifield (Eds.). *Migration theory: Talking across disciplines* (pp. 1–29). New York, NY: Routledge.

Brücker, H., Gil, S. E., McCormick, B., Saint-Paul, G., Venturini, A., & Zimmermann, K. F. (2002). Managing migration in the European welfare state. In T. Boeri, G. Hanson, & B. McCormick (Eds.), *Immigration policy and the welfare system: A report for the Fondazione Rodolfo Debenedetti* (pp. 1–168). Oxford: Oxford University Press.

Bygnes, S., & Erdal, M. B. (2017). Liquid migration, grounded lives: Considerations about future mobility and settlement among Polish and Spanish migrants in Norway. *Journal of Ethnic and Migration Studies*, 43(1), 102–118. doi:10.1080/1369183X.2016.1211004

Castles, S., de Haas, H., & Miller, M. J. (2014). *The age of migration: International population movements in the modern world* (5th ed.). Basingstoke: Palgrave Macmillan.

Cieslik, A. (2011). Where do you prefer to work? How the work environment influences return migration decisions from the United Kingdom to Poland. *Journal of Ethnic and Migration Studies*, 37(9), 1367–1383. doi:10.1080/1369183X.2011.623613

Cigagna, C., & Sulis, G. (2015). On the potential interaction between labour market institutions and immigration policies. *International Journal of Manpower*, 36(4), 441–468. Retrieved from https://doi.org/10.1108/IJM-11-2013-0259

Creese, G., Dyck, I., & McLaren, A. T. (2008). The "Flexible" immigrant? Human capital discourse, the family household and labour market strategies. *Journal of International Migration and Integration*, 9(3), 269–288. doi:10.1007/s12134-008-0061-0

De Cuyper, N., Bernhard-Oettel, C., Berntson, E., De Witte, H., & Alarco, B. (2008). Employability and employees' well-being: Mediation by job insecurity. *Applied Psychology: An International Review*, 57(3), 488–509. doi:10.1111/j.1464-0597.2008.00332.x

De Witte, H. (2005). Job insecurity: Review of the international literature on definitions, prevalence, antecedents and consequences. *SA Journal of Industrial Psychology*, 31(4), 1–6. doi:10.4102/sajip.v31i4.200

Dixon, J. C., Fullerton, A. S., & Robertson, D. L. (2013). Cross-national differences in workers' perceived job, labour market, and employment insecurity in Europe: Empirical tests and theoretical extensions. *European Sociological Review*,

29(5), 1053–1067. Retrieved from https://doi.org/10.1093/esr/jcs084

Drinkwater, S., & Garapich, M. P. (2015). Migrations strategies of polish migrants: Do they have any at all? *Journal of Ethnic and Migration Studies, 41*(12), 1909–1931. doi:10.1080/1369183X.2015.1027180

Edgell, S. (2006). *The sociology of work. Continuity and change in paid and unpaid work*. London: Sage Publications.

ESS Round 5: European Social Survey Round 5 Data. (2010). *Data file edition 3.4*. NSD – Norwegian Centre for Research Data, Norway – Data Archive and distributor of ESS data for ESS ERIC. Retrieved from https://doi.org/10.21338/NSD-ESS5-2010.

Eurofound. (2019). *European Working Conditions Survey 2015*. Retrieved from https://www.eurofound.europa.eu/data/european-working-conditions-survey

European Commission. (2007). *Towards common principles of flexicurity: More and better jobs through flexibility and security*. Brussels: COM/0359 final. Retrieved from https://eur-lex.europa.eu/LexUriServ/LexUriServ.do?uri=COM:2007:0359:FIN:EN:PDF

European Commission. (2011). *Special Eurobarometer 377: Employment and social policy*. Brussels: European Union Open Data Portal. Retrieved from http://ec.europa.eu/commfrontoffice/publicopinion/archives/ebs/ebs_377_en.pdf

Friberg, J. H. (2012). The stages of migration. From going abroad to settling down: Post-accession polish migrant workers in Norway. *Journal of Ethnic and Migration Studies, 38*(10), 1589–1605. doi:10.1080/1369183X.2012.711055

Galasińska, A., & Kozłowska, O. (2009). Discourses of a 'Normal Life' among Post-accession migrants from Poland to Britain. In K. Burrel (Ed.), *Polish migration to the UK in the 'New' European Union after 2004* (pp. 87–106). Farnham: Ashgate Publishing.

Gallie, D. (2017). The quality of work in a changing labour market. *Social Policy & Administration*, 51(2), 226–243. doi:10.1111/spol.12285

Gardawski, J., Bartkowski, J., Męcina, J., & Czarzasty, J. (2010). *Working poles and the crisis of Fordism*. Warsaw: Wydawnictwo Naukowe SCHOLAR.

Gaston, N., & Rajaguru, G. (2013). International migration and the welfare state revisited. *European Journal of Political Economy*, 29, 90–101.

Geis, W., Uebelmesser, S., & Werding, M. (2013). How do migrants choose their destination country? An analysis of institutional determinants. *Review of International Economics*, 21(5), 825–840. doi:10.1111/roie.12073

Glavin, P. (2013). The impact of job insecurity and job degradation on the sense of personal control. *Work and Occupations*, 40(2), 115–142. doi:10.1177/0730888413481031

Green, F. (2009). Subjective employment insecurity around the world. *Cambridge Journal of Regions, Economy and Society*, 2(3), 343–363. doi:10.1093/cjres/rsp003

Greenhalgh, L., & Rosenblatt, Z. (2010). Evolution of research on job security. *International Studies on Management & Organization*, 40(1), 6–19. doi:10.2753/IMO0020-8825400101

Grzymała-Kazłowska, A. (2018). From connecting to social anchoring: Adaptation and 'settlement' of Polish migrants in the UK. *Journal of Ethnic and Migration Studies*, *44*(2), 252–269. doi:10.1080/1369183X.2017.1341713

de Haas, H. (2011). *The Determinants of international migration: conceptualizing policy, origin and destination effects*. Retrieved from https://www.imi-n.org/publications/wp-32-11

Heery, E., & Salmon, J. (2000). *The insecure workforce*. New York, NY: Routledge.

Iglicka, K., & Gmaj, K. (2013). Circular migration patterns between Ukraine and Poland. In A. Triandafyllidou (Ed.), *Circular migration between Europe and its neighbourhood* (pp. 166–186). Oxford: Oxford University Press.

Kaczmarczyk, P. (2005). *Migracje zarobkowe Polaków w dobie przemian*. Warszawa: Wydawnictwa Uniwersytetu Warszawskiego.

Kaczmarczyk, P., & Kloc-Nowak, W. (2018). Teorie migracji. In M. Lesińska & M. Okólski (Eds.), *25 wykładów o migracjach* (pp. 47–67). Warszawa: Wydawnictwo Naukowe SCHOLAR.

Kalina-Prasznic, U. (2009). Wpływ globalizacji i integracji na zmiany rynku pracy. In M. Noga & M. K. Stawicka (Eds.), *Rynek pracy w Polsce w dobie integracji europejskiej i globalizacji* (pp. 7–14). Warszawa: CeDeWu.

Kalleberg, A. L. (2011). *Good jobs, bad jobs. The rise of polarized and precarious employment systems in the United States, 1970s to 2000s*. New York, NY: Russell Sage Foundation.

Kazlauskienė, A., & Rinkevičius, L. (2006). Lithuanian "brain drain" causes: Push and pull factors. *Engineering Economies*, 46(1), 27–37.

Kiersztyn, A. (2018). Non-standard employment and subjective insecurity: How can we capture job precarity using survey data? In A. L. Kalleberg & S. P. Vallas (Eds.), *Precarious work* (pp. 91–122). Bingley: Emerald Publishing Limited.

Kindler, M. (2011). *A risky business? Ukrainian migrant women in Warsaw's domestic work sector*. Amsterdam: Amsterdam University Press.

Kinnunen, U., Mauno, S., Nätti, J., & Happonen, M. (1999). Perceived job insecurity: A longitudinal study among finnish employees. *European Journal of Work and Organizational Psychology*, 8(2), 243–260. doi:10.1080/135943299398348

Kogan, I. (2007). *Working through barriers. Host country institutions and immigrant labour market performance in Europe*. Dordrecht: Springer.

Krasteva, V., McDonnell, A., & Tolgensbakk, I. (2019). Mobile young individuals: Subjective experiences of migration and return. In B. Hvinden, J. O'Reilly, M. A. Schoyen, & Ch. Hyggen (Eds.), *Negotiating early job insecurity. Well-being, scarring and resilience of European youth* (pp. 161–181). Cheltenham: Edward Elgar Publishing.

Kremer, M. (2016). Earned citizenship: Labour migrants' views on the welfare state. *Journal of Social Policy*, 45(3), 395–415. doi:10.1017/S0047279416000088

Kubitsky, J. (2012). *Psychologia migracji*. Warszawa: Difin.

Lee, E. (1966). A theory of migration. *Demography*, 3(1), 47–57.

Madsen, K. P. (1999). Denmark: Flexibility, security and labour market success. *ILO country employment policy review in selected OECD countries*. Geneva: International Labour Office.

Mai, Q. D. H. (2019). Precarious work in Europe: Assessing cross-national differences and institutional determinants of work precarity in 32 European countries. In A. L. Kalleberg & S. P. Vallas (Eds.), *Precarious work* (pp. 273–306). Bingley: Emerald Publishing Limited.

Marx, P. (2014). The effect of job insecurity and employability on preferences for redistribution in Western Europe. *Journal of European Social Policy*, 24(4), 351–366. doi:10.1177/0958928714538217

Mohr, G. B. (2000). The changing significance of different stressors after the announcement of bankruptcy: A longitudinal investigation with special emphasis on job insecurity. *Journal of Organizational Behavior*, 21(3), 337–359. doi:10.1002/(SICI)1099-1379(200005)21:3<337::AID-JOB18>3.0.CO;2-G

Muffels, R., Crouch, C., & Wilthagen, T. (2014). Flexibility and security: National social models in transitional labour markets. *Transfer: European Review of Labour and Research*, 20(1), 99–114. doi:10.1177/1024258913514361

Muffels, R., & Wilthagen, T. (2013). Flexicurity: A new paradigm for the analysis of labour markets and policies challenging the trade-off between flexibility and security. *Sociology Compass*, 7(2), 111–122. doi:10.1111/soc4.12014

Näswall, K., & De Witte, H. (2003). Who feels insecure in Europe? Predicting job insecurity from background variables. *Economic and Industrial Democracy*, 24(2), 189–215. Retrieved from https://doi.org/10.1177/0143831X030 24002003

Nowosielski, M. (2011). Growth and decline — The situation of Polish immigrant organizations in Germany. In M. Nowak & M. Nowosielski (Eds.), *(Post)transformational migration. Inequalities, welfare state, and horizontal mobility* (pp. 201–223). Frankfurt am Main: Peter Lang GmbH.

Parutis, V. (2014). "Economic migrants" or "middling transnationals"? East European migrants' experiences of work in the UK. *International Migration, 52*(1), 36–55. doi:10.1111/j.1468-2435.2010.00677.x

Piore, M. J. (1979). *Birds of passage: Migrant labor and industrial societies*. Cambridge: Cambridge University Press.

Pljevaljcic-Simkunas, D., & Thomsen, T. L. (2018). Precarious work? Migrants' narratives of coping with working conditions in the Danish labour market. *Central and Eastern Europe Migration Review, 7*(2), 35–51. doi:10.17467/ceemr.2018.09

Probst, M. T., & Jiang, L. (2017). European flexicurity policies: Multilevel effects on employee psychosocial reactions to job insecurity. *Safety Science, 100*(Part A), 83–90. doi:10.1016/j.ssci.2017.03.010

Pruijt, H., & Derogee, P. (2010). Employability and job security, friends or foes? The paradoxical reception of employacurity in the Netherlands. *Socio-Economic Review, 8*(2), 437–460. doi:10.1093/ser/mwq006

Razin, A., & Wahba, J. (2011). *Welfare magnet hypothesis, fiscal burden and immigration skill selectivity*. NBER Working Paper No. 17515. Retrieved from https://www.nber.org/papers/w17515.pdf

Skeldon, R. (1997). *Migration and development: A global perspective*. Harlow: Longman.

Ślusarczyk, M. (2019). *Transnarodowe życie rodzin na przykładzie polskich migrantów w Norwegii*. Kraków: Wydawnictwo Uniwersytetu Jagiellońskiego.

Standing, G. (2002). From people's security surveys to a decent work index. *International Labour Review, 141*(4), 441–454. doi:10.1111/j.1564-913X.2002.tb00248.x

Standing, G. (2011). *The precariat. The new dangerous class*. London: Bloomsbury Academic.

Stark, O. (1991). *The migration of labour*. Oxford: Basil Blackwell.

Strzelecki, P., Saczuk, K., Grabowska, I., & Kotowska, I. E. (2015). Rynek pracy. In J. Czapiński & T. Panek (Eds.), *Diagnoza Społeczna. Warunki i jakość życia Polaków* (pp. 129–173). Warszawa: Rada Monitoringu Społecznego.

Szczygielska, I. (2013). *Migracje zarobkowe kobiet i ich wpływ na funkcjonowanie rodzin*. Warszawa: Wydawnictwa Uniwersytetu Warszawskiego.

Vollmer, B. A. (2016). Ukrainian migration and the European Union. *Dynamics, subjectivity, and politics*. Basingstoke: Palgrave Macmillan.

White, A. (2017). *Polish families and migration since EU accession*. Bristol: Policy Press.

Xypolytas, N. (2017). The country of origin as a preparation stage: Towards a holistic approach to migrant exclusion. *International Journal of Sociology and Social Policy, 37*(13/14), 729–742. doi:10.1108/IJSSP-02-2017-0009

CHAPTER 2

ARE THE COUNTRIES DIFFERENT? STATISTICAL VIEW ON LABOUR MARKET SECURITY

Kamil Matuszczyk

INTRODUCTION

One of the main determinants of trends in international migrations are cross-country differences with respect to employment, in particular the persisting disparities in earnings. At the same time, countries tend to differ substantially as regards the various kinds of support instruments offered to workers, be it allowances, unemployment benefits, training or re-training facilitating search for employment. The form of such support depends largely on the dominant social model and economic capacities of a particular country. From labour migrants' viewpoint, the degree of access to all such allowances and benefits is important, and so are the rules of employment. Some countries offer more stable forms of employment, while in others those forms are less stable. It should be assumed that, when making decisions about the choice of a destination country, labour migrants will take into consideration both the level of earnings for the work they will perform and other elements comprising the construct of 'labour market security'.

The aim of the present chapter is a comparative analysis of labour markets and social security systems in four European countries, the United Kingdom, Germany, Poland and Ukraine, based on selected socio-economic indicators. An extensive comparison of both the subjective and objective situations of workers in the countries studied is offered. It is designed to provide a broad overview of the relevant differences among the four countries. Special attention is paid to the period between 2004 and 2017 and noticeable changes that occurred during that time as regards the situation in respective labour markets and the instruments of social security on offer. Using that information, an attempt is made to answer questions about the model of labour market security implemented and practised in each of the four states. It will thus be helpful in describing the determinants of labour market security that potentially influence the high waves of migration between Ukraine and Poland, as well as between Poland and, respectively, Germany and the United Kingdom. Because of the multitude and variety of indicators of the broadly conceived labour market conditions, used in different studies, we are limiting the ones we use to those having the greatest impact on the level of labour market security as defined earlier in this publication (see Fullerton, Robertson, & Dixon, 2011; Kiersztyn, 2018).

This study relies on different kinds of micro- and macro-level social indicators. The comparative analysis presented here is based on secondary data drawn from the databases of the Eurostat, the Organisation for Economic Cooperation and Development (OECD) as well as WSI Minimum Wage. Due to the fact that relevant comparative data for Ukraine are often lacking or incomplete (some comparative studies encompass European Union (EU) member states only), we also use the reports prepared by the State Statistics Service of Ukraine (SSSU) and the International Labour Organization (ILO). Unfortunately, there are still some gaps in our analyses, resulting from the unavailability of reliable data. Raw data on workers' subjective evaluations were extracted from the European Working Conditions Survey (EWCS) and the European Social Survey (ESS). The data used in the analyses that follow cover the period between 2004 and 2017. For some of the indicators, this enables us to track the changes in labour markets that have occurred following the EU enlargement by countries of Central and Eastern Europe, at times of the economic crisis of 2008 and, finally, during the political upheaval in Ukraine in 2014.

LABOUR MARKET SECURITY – SUBJECTIVE INDICATORS

Students of job, employment and income security often resort to analysing the data collected by major international social survey programs. Such data sets make comparisons between countries feasible; they also allow for tracking changes in the self-perceptions of the situation of workers over time. However, scholars who use the data from surveys such as, among others, the ESS or the EWCS, note that they are arguably imperfect. For instance, cultural bias affects the perceptions and meanings of the concept of 'security'. Also, conclusions are drawn based on a single survey item rather than a comprehensive reliable composite scale (Marx, 2014). Notwithstanding these objections, results obtained from survey data still constitute an important point of departure for the more nuanced in-depth analyses of the objective employment conditions experienced by workers in particular countries.

Discussing issues of work-related security, it is worth starting by answering the question about how important having a secure job actually is for workers. Perceptions of this issue can be analysed relying on the data from the ESS (2010 edition), in which respondents were asked what is important for them when looking for a job. It turns out that, out of five characteristics of employment, in three of the analysed countries a 'secure job' was selected most often as 'Very important' (Chart 1). In fact, 61.2% of German respondents answered this way. In Poland and the United Kingdom, the relevant fractions of respondents were equal to 56.4% and 45.1%, respectively. Only in Ukraine was 'high income' valued more highly than 'security', the former having been

Chart 1. Percentages of Respondents Answering 'Very Important' to the Question: 'For You Personally, How Important Do You Think Each of the Following Would Be If You Were Choosing a Job?' — As of 2010.

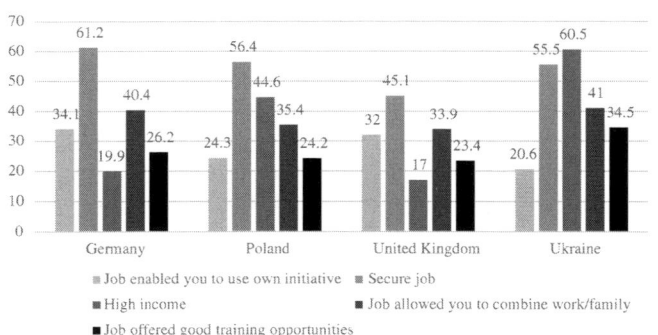

Source: Author's own elaboration based on ESS Round 5: European Social Survey Round 5 Data (2010).

pointed to by more than 60% and the latter by 55.5% of respondents. Overall, the proportions of particular answers differ especially between Germany and the United Kingdom, suggesting workers' divergent expectations as regards labour markets.

In the context of labour market security, workers' opinions regarding the perspectives of maintaining their current employment in future, that is, job insecurity, are also worth studying. That dimension was measured within the framework of a three past editions of the EWCS (2005, 2010, and 2015). It turns out that, from the pan-European perspective, the percentage of workers anxious about losing their jobs had increased considerably in the period 2005–2010, that is, the period marked by an economic crisis, to remain stable afterwards (Chart 2). However, a closer look at the situations of Poland, Germany and the United Kingdom leads to uncovering substantial disparities within the set of the three states. Over the years between 2005 and 2010,

Chart 2. Employed Persons (Aged 15–64) Expecting a Possible Loss of Their Job in the Next Six Months as of 2005, 2010 and 2015.

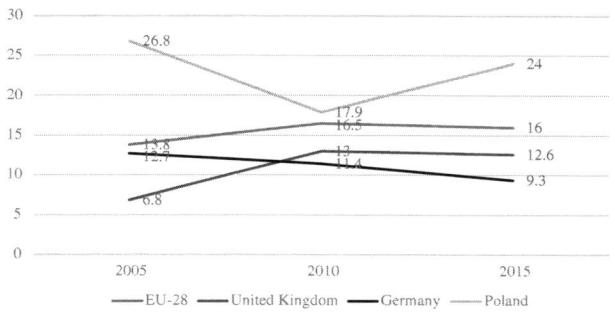

Source: Author's own elaboration based on Eurostat (2019a).

respondents' evaluations in this respect got more pessimistic in the United Kingdom and more optimistic in Poland, while in Germany no substantial change was observed. At the same time, despite having declined, the percentage of Poles anxious about losing jobs was higher than in the two other EU countries analysed. In the following years, we again dealt with great differences. In the period 2010–2015, the evaluations of German and British respondents remained stable, whereas in Poland the work-related anxiety increased. The trends being observed in the three countries thus seem to be entirely distinctive. Poland still is a setting where the experience of a fear of losing a job is most common. Such anxiety is relatively rare in the United Kingdom, a sign of a loss of a job not being considered a traumatic event, perhaps because of the chances of finding new employment quickly being objectively high. In the case of Poland, the apparent increase in the anxiety of losing a job is echoed by the results of other research efforts. For example, Kurowska (2017) observes that within the 2010–2015 period every second worker in Poland experienced a decreasing sense of security of employment.

The level of job security is also directly associated with the concerns about remaining unemployed for a prolonged or even indefinite period of time. In two editions of the ESS (2008 and 2016), respondents were asked about their perceptions of the probability of becoming unemployed and looking for work within the next 12 months. Over the period between 2008 and 2016, a noticeable positive shift in respondents' subjective assessments occurred (Table 1). For example, in 2008, 14.1% (i.e. answers 'likely' and 'very likely') of the German sample expected a loss of work, and in 2016 the proportion dropped to 9.5%. The corresponding figures in the years 2008 and 2016, respectively, were equal to 16.4% and 12.8% for the British sample and to 17.4% and 15.4% for the Polish one. This trend toward more

Are the Countries Different?

Table 1. Percentages of Respondents Answering to the Question: 'How Likely It Is that during the Next 12 months You Will Be Unemployed and Looking for Work for At Least Four Consecutive Weeks?' – As of 2008 and 2016.

	Not at All Likely		Not Very Likely		Likely		Very Likely		Not Working/Not Looking for Work/ Never Worked	
	2008	2016	2008	2016	2008	2016	2008	2016	2008	2016
Germany	33.7	49.1	26.8	24.0	7.8	5.3	6.3	4.2	25.3	17.5
Poland	17.1	13.3	25.7	29.0	12.2	11.4	5.2	4.0	39.8	42.4
United Kingdom	37.8	43.5	29.7	27.0	10.4	7.5	6.0	5.3	16.1	16.6
Ukraine	6.5	*	14.1	*	19.8	*	10.9	*	48.8	*

Source: Author's own elaboration based on ESS Round 4: European Social Survey Round 4 Data (2008) and ESS Round 8: European Social Survey Round 8 Data (2016).

Note: *Lack of data series.

optimism can perhaps be explained pointing to general feelings of optimism at times of recovery after the economic crisis. Comparative data for Ukraine are unfortunately lacking as the country participated in the survey in 2008 only. At that time 30% of Ukrainian respondents feared a job loss and being unemployed within the following 12 months. It should perhaps be expected that, due to the very difficult economic situation in the country and the resulting emigration processes, the situation in this respect has not improved considerably since then.

Employment security is another indicator used to measure workers' perceptions of their own situation in a labour market. It allows respondents for presenting their attitudes with respect to the situation in the labour market in case they lose their jobs. The analysis of that indicator echoes previous figures. According to these, workers in the United Kingdom tend to enjoy the highest levels of self-perceived employment security (Table 2). Every second respondent in that country acknowledged that in the event of losing his/her current

Table 2. Percentages of Respondents Answering to the Question: 'If I Were to Lose or Quit My Current Job, It Would Be Easy for Me to Find a Job of Similar Salary' – As of 2015.

	United Kingdom	Germany	Poland
Agree	49	39	34
Disagree	35	39	35
Neither agree nor disagree	16	23	32

Source: Author's own elaboration based on Eurofound (2019a).

employment they would have no major trouble finding a similar work, remunerated similarly. In Germany and Poland, the percentages of positive answers to this question were substantially lower (39% and 34%, respectively).

And yet, an important caveat should be added to what was said above. Namely, the perceived level of employment security varies depending on the kind of work performed. In particular, the analysis by Chung (2015, p. 292) demonstrates that, regardless of the macro-level context, those performing simple mundane works, employed in basic services and low-skilled occupations, are characterised by higher self-perceived levels of employment insecurity than those placed higher on the occupational stratification ladder (i.e. managers and professionals).

Additional relevant information concerning the perceived level of employment security in the countries selected for our analysis can be extracted from the 2010 edition of the ESS. During that edition, respondents were asked a question regarding the degree of ease/difficulty in finding another job. The data collected for that question suggest that in Germany and Ukraine workers were subject to a relatively high self-perceived level of employment insecurity (**Table 3**). In both these countries, nearly one in five respondents maintained that in case of a job loss it would be extremely difficult for him/her to find similar employment. In Poland and the United Kingdom, the corresponding percentages were much lower.

Taken together, figures presented in **Tables 2 and 3** seem to indicate the relatively low prevalence of fear of losing a job in the United Kingdom, a country where the opportunity of finding alternative (comparable) employment tends to be quite high.

The level of income security experienced by workers in a particular country has thus far been analysed relatively rarely, despite its being no less important than job or

Table 3. Percentages of Respondents Answering to the Question: 'How Difficult or Easy Would It Be for You to Get a Similar or Better Job with Another Employer If You Had to Leave Your Current Job?' – As of 2010.

	Extremely Difficult	1	2	3	4	5	6	7	8	9	Extremely Easy
Germany	17.5	8.4	12.5	11.2	5.2	16.3	6.1	7.0	8.3	3.3	4.3
Poland	6.4	8.5	12.1	10.6	9.3	17.0	9.9	10.5	10.5	2.7	2.5
United Kingdom	4.1	7.3	10.3	10.5	8.9	14.1	10.7	12.5	13.3	4.1	4.1
Ukraine	18.7	10.1	11.1	10.3	7.2	17.0	7.4	6.2	4.2	2.5	5.2

Source: Author's own elaboration based on ESS Round 5: European Social Survey Round 5 Data (2010).

employment security. As a part of two of the ESS editions (2008 and 2016), a question has been asked enabling us to examine the degree of respondents' anxiety as regards income, be it from either work or other sources. In 2008, the highest degree of income insecurity was expressed by the Ukrainian respondents, 35.9% of whom believed that the probability of obtaining income insufficient for covering all necessary household expenses in the following 12 months was high (Table 4). Due to the unavailability of adequate post-2012 survey data for Ukraine, we are unable to evaluate systematically the potential change in Ukrainians' subjective assessments of the issues we study here. It can be fairly safely assumed, however, that no significant shift towards more optimism has occurred. On the other side of the spectrum, it is the German sample that is characterised by the highest evaluations of income security; only one in 10 respondents expressed the anxiety that they would obtain an income too low to cover the expenses of a 'normal' existence. In comparison to 2008, the proportion of such persons has dropped by more than 4% (i.e. those choosing the answers 'likely' and 'very likely'). As long as the British respondents are considered, the corresponding proportions amounted to 30.7% and 20.3% in 2008 and 2016, respectively. Finally, Poland appears to have seen the greatest positive change in this respect, the proportion of the least optimistic answers having dwindled by more than 15 percentage points. Nevertheless, in comparison to Germany and the United Kingdom, the prevalence of anxiety as regards future incomes was still relatively high.

Our inspection of the aforementioned subjective indicators for the years 2005–2016 has largely confirmed significant cross-country differences in worker opinions as regards their individual situations in labour markets. The core assumption underlying our work, maintaining that workers in the United

Table 4. Percentages of Respondents Answering to the Question: 'During the Next 12 Months How Likely Is It that There Will Be Some Periods When You Don't Have Enough Money to Cover Your Household Necessities?' – as of 2008 and 2016.

	Not at All Likely		Not Very Likely		Likely		Very Likely	
	2008	2016	2008	2016	2008	2016	2008	2016
Germany	37.7	50.5	46.5	37.9	11.7	8.1	4.2	3.5
Poland	10.9	22.7	48.6	52.0	32.1	21.0	8.4	4.2
United Kingdom	28.3	39.0	41.0	40.7	20.4	14.5	10.3	5.8
Ukraine	2.6	*	16.0	*	45.5	*	35.9	*

Source: Author's own elaboration based on ESS Round 4: European Social Survey Round 4 Data (2008) and ESS Round 8: European Social Survey Round 8 Data (2016).

Note: *Lack of data series.

Kingdom enjoy a considerably higher level of employment security than their than those working and leaving in Germany thus seems substantiated. In Germany, by contrast, workers have much better perspectives for keeping the current employment (i.e. high job security). At the same time, we should emphasise the pronounced positive change which has taken place in Poland within just over 10 years. Nevertheless, a large number of workers in Poland still look into future with a degree of fear, which may be a factor behind the persisting high level of emigration.

LABOUR MARKET SECURITY – OBJECTIVE INDICATORS

Unemployment and Social Expenditures for the Unemployed

The extant literature on the topic tends to argue that a country's unemployment rate has an impact on workers' subjective evaluations and opinions with regard to their labour market security (Chung & van Oorschot, 2011; Fullerton et al., 2011; Marx, 2014). That means both job security and employment security are strongly correlated with the probability of a job loss and being unemployed. In general, the higher the unemployment rate, the higher the prevalence of the fear of a job loss, (job insecurity) and, obviously, the smaller the perceived probability of finding a new employment (employment insecurity).

In the years between 2004 and 2017, the unemployment rate in the four countries examined had undergone dynamic changes (**Chart 3**). The greatest scope of change was observed in Poland. At the time of that country's accession to the EU, that is, in 2004, the proportion of the unemployed among

Chart 3. Unemployment Rate (Aged 15–74) as of 2004–2017.

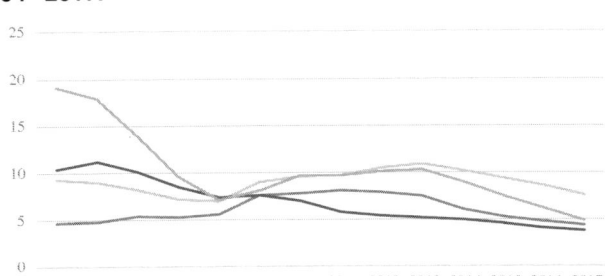

Source: Author's own elaboration based on Eurostat (2019b).

those economically active amounted to nearly 20%. Following a period of fluctuation in the years 2008–2011 (i.e. during the economic crisis), the unemployment rate started to go down rapidly to reach the level of 5% in 2017. The most recent statistical data (2017) show that the unemployment rate for all the three EU member states examined here remains below the average for EU-28. The scale of unemployment in Poland, Germany and the United Kingdom thus remains within the limits of the so-called 'frictional unemployment'. This means that a low unemployment rate can be achieved under both the socio-economic model emphasising job security and the one that is based on employment security. At the same time, the comparative cross-country analyses suggest that the United Kingdom is the setting where the (low) unemployment rate is least prone to temporal fluctuations.

In Ukraine, the unemployment rate remained nearly constant between 2004 and 2017. In spite of the economic crisis of 2008 and the political crisis of 2014, the unemployment rate for that country did never exceed 10%. In 2004, 8.6% of the population aged 15–70 remained without employment, whereas in 2017 the unemployment rate reached 9.5% (SSSU, 2018). Yet, we should be aware that in Ukraine we deal with a substantial extent of the so-called 'hidden unemployment'.

Remaining without work for certain periods of time in the course of one's occupational career seems to have become a norm in the era of post-Fordism. Despite the decreasing unemployment rates, periods without employment are a serious challenge for both the unemployed and those designing labour market policies. The chance of eventually finding a job tends to decline as the length of time one remains unemployed increases. Residents of the United Kingdom seem to in the best position in this respect, as 40% of those who become unemployed at some point in their lives find a new job within a period of two months (**Chart 4**). This upside of the British labour market is robust to time passage and various changes it brings. The period between 2004 and 2017 brought Poland a dramatic improvement in this respect, albeit still only 30% of the unemployed find a new job within two months following the loss of the previous one. In Germany, a positive change occurred as well, even if to a lesser degree than in Poland. At the same time, the percentage of the unemployed getting rid of this status within two months is lower than the corresponding figure for the United Kingdom.

The situation in Ukraine is substantially worse than in the three EU countries examined. In 2017, the average length of a period of unemployment was equal to seven months. One in four unemployed persons (26.7%) in Ukraine faces prolonged or permanent unemployment (i.e. lasting over 12 months) (SSSU, 2018).

Chart 4. Duration of Unemployment (Aged 15–74) in Months as of 2004 and 2017.

	EU-28 (2004)	EU-28 (2017)	Germany (2004)	Germany (2017)	Poland (2004)	Poland (2017)	United Kingdom (2004)	United Kingdom (2017)
<1	6.7	8.4	5.5	11.6	1.9	16.1	15.8	16.5
1–2	13.6	15.8	11.5	16.2	7.6	13.2	24.9	24
3–5	15.6	14.5	15.2	14.1	14.4	22.1	19.6	16.1
6–11	18.5	15.1	15.7	15.4	22.4	17.5	17.3	16
12–17	12.2	11.4	11	8.5	18.4	13.9	7.6	8.2
18–23	6.7	5.5	8.2	6.5	9.6	4.4	5.5	3.7
24–47	14.3	13.5	14.5	11.3	19.6	8.7	5.5	6.7
>48	11.4	14.5	16.9	15.3	6.1	4.1	4.8	7.3

■ <1 ■ 1–2 ■ 3–5 ■ 6–11 ■ 12–17 ■ 18–23 ■ 24–47 ■ >48 ■ not started ■ no response

Source: Author's own calculation based on Eurostat (2019c).

The amounts of public expenditures allocated for the purpose of supporting the unemployed have an overwhelmingly strong impact on their daily lives. The mere awareness of the existence of the advanced systems of public support for the unemployed relieves workers from much of the stress caused by periodic economic downturns and the associated deterioration of labour market conditions (Boeri & van Ours, 2008). In spite of the recent decline in unemployment support expenditures, Germany continues to be the leader as regards public spending in this area (**Table 5**), easily overtaking the United Kingdom. Poland, on the contrary, occupies the opposite side of the spectrum as one of the EU countries spending least on support for the unemployed.

Table 5. Expenditures on Unemployment in Purchasing Power Standard Per Inhabitant as of 2004, 2008, 2012 and 2016.

	2004	2008	2012	2016
UE-28	*	325.79	405.52	368.73
United Kingdom	161.47	155.64	185.29	109.11
Germany	587.23	425.87	387.29	371.47
Poland	77.25	53.92	56.09	38.86

Source: Author's own elaboration based on Eurostat (2019d).
Note: *Data for EU-15.

THE ECONOMIC WELL-BEING OF WORKERS

The economic situation in a given labour market is determined primarily by the level of earnings. Ideally, not only should the income earned allow for satisfying one's essential needs, but it should also enable one to improve his/her qualifications and accumulate savings. These can then serve as a safety net of income security in case of unemployment. Amounts of income obtained from work are among the most strongly differentiating criteria when it comes to the evaluation of the conditions of employment in particular EU states. It turns out that in the period 2005–2017 the greatest relative increase (by over 132%) in median annual income, measured in purchasing power standard (PPS), was registered in Poland (an increase from 4,759 to 11,059) (Chart 5). In the United Kingdom, where the median income in 2017 was equal to 18,043, a small relative increase, by no more than 7%, was observed. Germany enjoys the highest median

Chart 5. Median Income in PPS between 2005 and 2017.

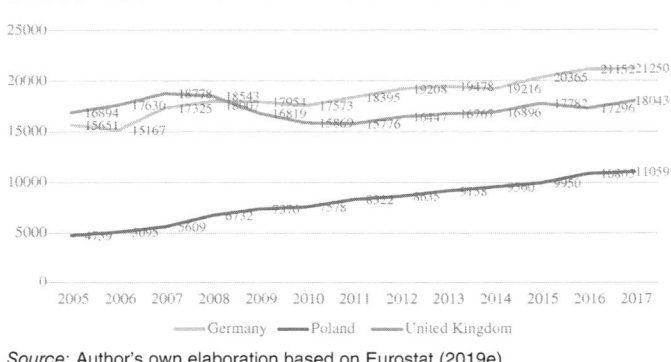

Source: Author's own elaboration based on Eurostat (2019e).

income, having amounted to 21,250 in 2017, twice as high as in Poland and by 17% higher than in the United Kingdom.

From the data collected by the ILO (2013), it can be concluded that between 2004 and 2011 a systematic increase in median income was registered in Ukraine, albeit it was accompanied by high inflation.

The regulations with respect to minimum wages constitute an important instrument of labour market policy, influencing the sense of security of the workers resident in a particular country. As of 2017, minimum wage regulations were in force in 22 out of 28 EU member states. Other allowances and social benefits which workers and the unemployed are entitled to depend on the minimum wage level. Of the four countries examined here, the highest minimum wage is in effect in Germany (data for 2017),[1] being equal to 8.84 per hour in Euro. The British minimum wage is somewhat lower, 7.86 per hour in Euro, while for Poland it drops considerably, that is, to the level of 2.71 in Euro. Ukraine, has the lowest minimum wage, just 0.60 in Euro (WSI Minimum Wage Database, 2019).

At the same time, it is worth emphasising that the proportions of workers receiving minimum wages may differ substantially between countries. For example, applying the Eurostat methodology, defining 'persons earning minimum wages' as those with a monthly wage below the value of 105% of the legal minimum wage, workers residing in Poland were three times as likely as those residing in the United Kingdom to earn a minimum wage only (4% and 12%, respectively) (Eurostat, 2019k). A comprehensive comparison is not possible here due to the lack of appropriate data for Germany and Ukraine.

Another indicator measuring the differentiation within the group of employees is the proportion of low-wage earners, a group encompassing employees (excluding apprentices) earning two-thirds or less of the national median gross hourly wage.[2] The available data suggest that the proportion of low-wage earners in the United Kingdom, Germany and Poland is roughly the same (Table 6). In the years 2006–2014, no significant change had occurred in this respect in those three countries. For example, in 2014, every fourth employee in

Table 6. Low-wage Earners as a Proportion of All Employees (Excluding Apprentices) in Companies Employing 10 or More Employees as of 2006, 2010 and 2014.

	2006	2010	2014
EU-28	-	16.96	17.19
United Kingdom	21.77	22.06	21.26
Germany	20.3	22.24	22.48
Poland	24.72	24.16	23.56

Source: Author's own elaboration based on Eurostat (2019f).

Poland as well as every fifth in both the United Kingdom and Germany received wages lower than or equal to two-thirds of the national median gross hourly earnings.

In addition to the amount of income obtained, it is the dynamics of the changes in wages that has an impact on labour market security. As it turns out, in Poland, the United Kingdom and Germany, the proportion of workers whose salary or income decreased in the last 12 months had dropped between 2010 and 2015 (Table 7). At the same time, in Germany and the United Kingdom, a significantly greater group of employees recorded an increase in salaries.

Unfortunately, comparable data for Ukraine are not available. In this context, it should be pointed out that in that country there is a great proportion of workers employed in the 'grey zone' of the economy, dominated by illegal or semi-legal work (Round, Williams, & Rodgers, 2008, p. 159). According to the SSSU (2018), in 2017, nearly every fourth worker (22.9%) was in informal employment. Of those 43% were in

Table 7. Percentages of Respondents Answering to the Question: 'Has Your Salary or Income Changed in the Last 12 Months/Past Year?' in 2010 and 2015.

	United Kingdom		Germany		Poland	
	2010	2015	2010	2015	2010	2015
Decrease	14	8	10	4	14	8
Increase	36	42	27	44	26	24
No change	50	50	64	53	60	68

Source: Author's own elaboration based on Eurofound (2019a) and Eurofound (2019b).

formal sector enterprises and 57% in informal sector enterprises. At the same time, the authors of the ILO report (2013) note the minimal proportion of employees in Ukraine who are deprived of social protection, namely those employed on civil law contracts. Between 2004–2011, this amounted to 1–2%.

WORKERS' EMPLOYABILITY

Raising qualifications and gaining new skills is becoming a very important element in enhancing chances for obtaining the first and subsequent jobs. This is why maintaining a high level of employability by the employees is highly advisable. In order to ensure it, labour market policies should aim at guaranteeing workers good conditions for re-training as well as raising or updating qualifications through systems of both formal and informal education. The analyses above indicate that the scope of active labour market policy (ALMP) (Chung & van Oorschot, 2011), implemented in a given country, has a strong positive impact on both the aggregate level of employment and individual professional careers. The most generous public expenditures on ALMP in 2015, relative to a country's GDP, were allocated by Germany (0.63%) followed by Poland (0.46%) and the United Kingdom (0.23%) (OECD, 2019b). At the same time, it is worth noting that it is the United Kingdom where employees switch jobs most often (Eurobarometer, 2011). The employees interviewed there reported to have switched jobs 4.4 times on average, the EU average being 3.2 times. Employees in Germany and Poland changed employers far less often than those in the United Kingdom, on average 2.8 times in their working life to date (Eurobarometer, 2011).

Another indicator important in the context of employability is workers' participation in both formal and informal

Table 8. Employed Persons (Aged 15–64) Participating in Job-related Non-formal Education and Training in the Past 12 Months in 2005, 2010 and 2015.

	2005	2010	2015
EU-28	26.4	34.0	39.0
United Kingdom	39.1	45.7	50.6
Germany	25.3	37.1	41.7
Poland	26.5	33.4	35.5

Source: Author's own elaboration based on Eurostat (2019g).

job-related education and training. As follows from Table 8, there is a distinguishable general trend towards greater participation of employees in various forms of training aimed at raising their job-related qualifications. Of the three EU countries under analysis, the highest level of participation in such training was observed in the United Kingdom where every second working respondent to a survey conducted in 2015 claimed to have participated in job-related non-formal education and training. In Germany and Poland, the corresponding figures exceeded 41% and 35%, respectively.

TYPE OF CONTRACT AND QUALITY OF EMPLOYMENT

The types of contracts offered workers in a particular country constitute yet another indicator commonly used in the analyses of the objective dimension of work-related security (Berloffa, Matteazzi, Şandor, & Villa, 2016; Kiersztyn, 2018). The greatest danger of losing a job is faced by agency workers and fixed-contract employees (Klandermans, Hesselink, & van Vuuren, 2010).

Are the Countries Different?

The growing prevalence of non-standard forms of employment (i.e. part-time, quasi self-employment) and other temporary contracts has been accompanied by a decline in standards of social protection and a spread of labour market insecurity (Balz, 2017; Dieckhoff, Gash, Mertens, & Romeu-Gordo, 2015). In this context, the indicator commonly applied for measuring the objective level of employee security is the proportion of workers on part-time contracts. That type of employment is much more prevalent in Germany than in the United Kingdom or Poland (Chart 6). However, it should be noted that in the two former countries part-time employment is most often a means of addressing the necessity of taking care of children or disabled adults. Thus, that form of employment makes work–life balance possible. In Poland, low wages tend to substantially reduce employees' interest in part-time employment. In most cases, part-time employment does simply not bring an income sufficient to satisfy essential needs. In this

Chart 6. Employed Persons by Full-time/Part-time Activity in 2008 and 2017.

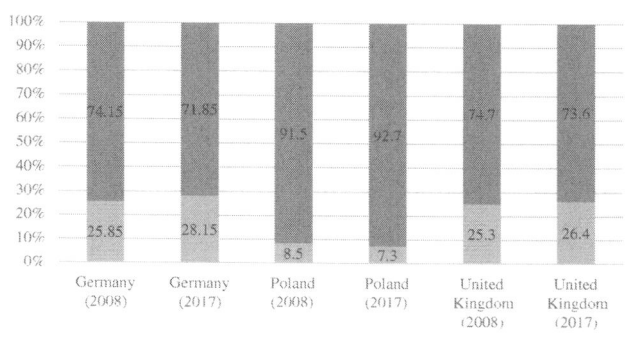

Source: Author's own calculation based on Eurostat (2019h).

context, it should be emphasised, however, that scholars are not unanimous in equating part-time employment with worse conditions of employment, especially in cases marked by labour market instability (Balz, 2017; Keune, 2015, p. 378).

Apart from the type of contract, any analysis of varying approaches to labour market security should take into consideration the issue of job tenure. The analysis by Berglund, Furåker, and Vulkan (2014, p. 179) has largely confirmed that the longer people stay with an employer, the more likely they are to perceive the risk of losing their jobs as low. Aggregate data for EU member states indicate that in the years 2002–2012 the average job tenure grew from 116.5 months to 123 months (Bachmann & Felder, 2018). Of the countries analysed here, the United Kingdom is the setting with the lowest percentage of persons maintaining employment in one workplace for over 60 months (Chart 7). In

Chart 7. Employment in Current Job by Duration (in Months) as of 2005 and 2017.

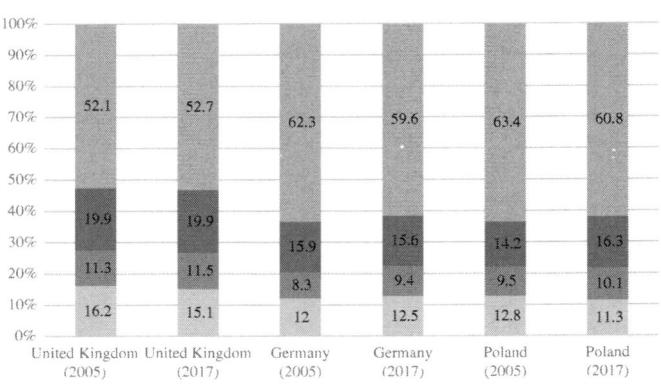

■ 0–11 ■ 12–23 ■ 24–59 ■ 60 or over

Source: Author's own elaboration based on Eurostat (2019i).

Poland and Germany, the proportions of such persons were about 8−10 percentage points higher. This again indicates that the British labour market is characterised by greater internal mobility than its German and Polish counterparts.

EMPLOYMENT PROTECTION LEGISLATION AND POSITION OF TRADE UNIONS

The issue of labour market security is playing a fundamental role in the period of economic recession and the associated unemployment surges. Large-scale layoffs trigger off a sense of danger among workers. This is why numerous states decide to develop support systems for both employees at a high risk of a job loss and the unemployed. Furthermore, states may choose to act in such a way as to prevent an uncontrolled growth of unemployment rates, implementing instruments of support for employers and thereby incentivising them to refrain from downsizing. Although employment protection legislation (EPL) is a guarantee for employees, especially in the context of job security, the extant literature emphasises a growing differentiation in this respect. This results from the apparent increase in the proportion of employees not covered by protection laws, including those hired under contracts regulated by legislation other than the respective labour codes (Barbieri & Cutuli, 2016). The literature on the topic thus repeatedly emphasises the causal link between EPL and issues of the stability of employment, unemployment rates and, last but not least, the flows of employees within labour markets (Boeri & van Ours, 2008; Kwiatkowski & Włodarczyk, 2017).

Based on the OECD data (**Table 9**), we can draw a conclusion that the United Kingdom has the most liberal EPL. Germany occupies a position on the opposite side of the

Table 9. Levels of Employment Protection in OECD Indices of 2013 and 2014, with Scale from 0 (Least Restrictions) to 6 (Most Restrictions).

	Protection of Permanent Workers against Individual and Collective Dismissals	Protection of Permanent Workers against (Individual) Dismissal	Specific Requirements for Collective Dismissal	Regulation on Temporary Forms of Employment
Germany	2.84	2.53	3.63	1.75
Poland	2.39	2.20	2.88	2.33
United Kingdom	1.59	1.18	2.63	0.54

Source: Author's own elaboration based on OECD (2019a).

spectrum, this type of regulations being fundamental for the functioning of the labour market there. Poland is somewhere in-between. It is worth noting that in all the three countries under study it is collective redundancies that is subject to the most demanding and rigid protection rules.

When analysing the issues of labour market security, we should also not neglect the role of the labour market institutions, especially trade unions. Mass survey data tend to confirm that properly working institutions have a positive effect on the general level of employment stability (Ogbonnaya, Gahan, & Eib, 2019). A special role is attributed to trade unions and their commitment to the protection of workers' rights (Keune, 2015). A country's high level of unionisation and a non-negligible bargaining power of trade unions in trilateral negotiations generally translate into a relatively high level of workers' protection. Obviously, this applies especially to those who happen to be trade union members (Esser & Olsen, 2012; Kiersztyn, 2018). Moreover, under the socio-economic model based on employment security, the overall role of trade unions is relatively minor, even if it does not necessarily mean a lower level of unionisation. Unlike in Germany and Poland, trade unions in the United Kingdom are focused solely on the protection of individual workers rather than simultaneously trying to accomplish various political goals (Keune, 2015).

PRECARIOUS EMPLOYMENT

Another important issue worth taking into consideration here is the so-called 'precarious employment'. In a nutshell, the term refers to the kind of employment which, in practice, does not bring one labour market security, but is unavoidable as the only means of either gaining essential professional experience or obtaining income necessary simply to survive (Standing, 2011). The scale of this sort of employment can be measured by the percentage of employees for whom the duration of work contracts did not exceed three months.[3] Comparative data covering the period between 2009 and 2017 suggest that the prevalence of 'precarious employment' was very low in all the three EU states examined in this chapter. In Germany and the United Kingdom, the proportion of those in such employment was equal to just about 1%. The corresponding figures for Poland were considerably higher, albeit never exceeding 5%. This points to a marginal role of this type of low-quality employment in the context of the three aforementioned national economies (Chart 8).

Chart 8. Precarious Employment (% of Employment Aged 15–64) as of 2009–2017.

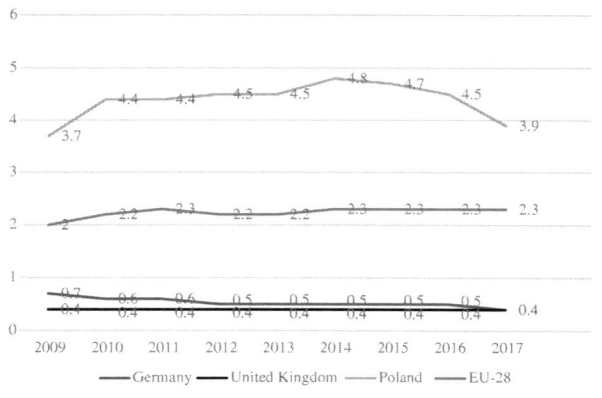

Source: Author's own elaboration based on Eurostat (2019j).

SUMMARY

The current analysis of both the subjective perceptions of workers and the objective determinants that affect the levels of their labour market security largely confirms our research theses. Despite implementing divergent socio-economic models and social policy instruments, Germany and the United Kingdom seem to have reached similar (high) levels of labour market security. Comparable unemployment rates and wage levels, in addition to equally optimistic subjective perceptions of security as expressed by residents of those two states, have been arrived at based on radically different 'recipes'. Clearly, Germany has chosen the strategy of job security, while the United Kingdom sticks to the employment security model. The above thesis seems to be supported by various indicators, such as the frequency of job switching or the length of tenure with the same employer. On the subjective side, employees in the United Kingdom are less anxious about a potential job loss as they perhaps believe that they can find another one relatively fast. By contrast, in Germany, legislation protecting workers from layoffs and guaranteeing state-funded support in case of unemployment is highly valued. In the context of the notion of 'flexicurity', we can say that in the United Kingdom an emphasis is put on flexibility, while in Germany it is security that is prioritised. The situation in Poland is still rather mixed, albeit with a predominance of flexibility, but certain improvements in the area of labour relations and an overall increase in labour market security should be noticed there as well. While acknowledging the advantages of secure jobs, employees in Poland feel, to a great extent, insecure about maintaining the job they have or finding another one. The issue of income security definitely dominates the debate on the prevalence of job security over employment security or vice versa. On the one hand, Polish government guarantees a high level of protection against layoffs, showing an approach inspired by the model in effect in Germany. On the other hand, however, it tolerates the existence of a segment of the labour market where flexible forms of employment prevail. State-funded support for the employees at times of transition between employers is also limited and, as such, it does not compare to what is offered by the British or the German state.

The situation in Ukraine is difficult to interpret and summarise, mainly because we have limited data at our disposal. As a country from outside the EU, it does not participate in some of the surveys and research projects carried out by the Eurostat, the Eurobarometer or the OECD. The available data, incomplete and imperfect as they are, suggest that security is a relatively rare state for the participants of the Ukrainian labour market. Low wages, high proportion of jobs in the 'grey zone' of the economy, as well as ineffective, even if formally well-developed, labour protection legislation, all contribute to a high level of insecurity and thereby foster emigration.

Overall, our analysis of the situation in labour markets of the four European countries largely confirms the assumptions put forward thus far, related to the directions of migrations and the impact of labour market security on migration-related decisions. Ukraine is a country of purely emigration. Regarding Poland, a rise in wages, a low unemployment rate and a growing scope of social benefits appear to be the factors behind a change of the status of that country from its being a typical country of emigration to one of both emigration and immigration. However, the generally negative subjective evaluations of the Polish labour market by Polish citizens perhaps contribute to the persistence of high levels of emigration. On the migration map, the United Kingdom and Germany are definitely countries of immigration, albeit they attract different categories of immigrants. In the former country, immigrants should expect less stability and be willing to respond to the requirements of employers. In Germany, on the contrary, migrants can count on more stable conditions of employment. Nevertheless, the effects in the form of labour market security, defined in terms of income security, tend to be remarkably similar in both these countries.

NOTES

1. Data in purchasing power parities (PPP) are available for 2018: Germany — 8.52, United Kingdom — 7.46, Poland — 5.29 and Ukraine — 3.27. Source: WSI Minimum Wage Database (2019a).

2. https://ec.europa.eu/eurostat/cache/metadata/en/earn_ses_main_esms.htm

3. https://ec.europa.eu/eurostat/web/products-eurostat-news/-/DDN-20180209-1

REFERENCES

Bachmann, R., & Felder, R. (2018). Job stability in Europe over the cycle. *International Labour Review*, *157*(3), 481–518. doi:10.1111/ilr.12117

Balz, A. (2017). Cross-national variations in the security gap: Perceived job insecurity among temporary and permanent employees and employment protection legislation. *European Sociological Review*, *33*(5), 675–692. doi:10.1093/esr/jcx067

Barbieri, P., & Cutuli, G. (2016). Employment protection legislation, labour market dualism, and inequality in Europe. *European Sociological Review*, *32*(4), 501–516. doi:10.1093/esr/jcv058

Berglund, T., Furåker, B., & Vulkan, P. (2014). Is job insecurity compensated for by employment and income security? *Economic and Industrial Democracy*, *35*(1), 165−184. doi:10.1177/0143831X12468904

Berloffa, G., Matteazzi, E., Şandor, A., & Villa, P. (2016). Youth employment security and labour market institutions: A dynamic perspective. *International Labour Review*, *155*(4), 651−678. doi:10.1111/ilr.12034

Boeri, T., & van Ours, J. (2008). *The economics of imperfect labor markets*. Princeton, NJ: Princeton University Press.

Chung, H. (2015). Subjective employment insecurity gap between occupations: Variance across Europe. In W. Eichhorst & P. Marx (Eds.), *Non-standard employment in post-industrial labour markets. An occupational perspective* (pp. 271−297). Cheltenham: Edward Elgar Publishing.

Chung, H., & van Oorschot, W. (2011). Institutions versus market forces: Explaining the employment insecurity pf European individuals during (the beginning of) the financial crisis. *Journal of European Social Policy*, *21*(4), 287−301. doi:10.1177/0958928711412224

Dieckhoff, M., Gash, V., Mertens, A., & Romeu-Gordo, L. (2015). Female atypical employment in the service occupations: A comparative study of time trends in Germany and the UK. In W. Eichhorst & P. Marx (Eds.), *Non-standard employment in post-industrial labour markets. An occupational perspective* (pp. 353−377). Cheltenham: Edward Elgar Publishing.

ESS Round 4: European Social Survey Round 4 Data. (2008). Data archive and distributor of ESS data for ESS ERIC. Data file edition 4.5. Norwegian Centre for Research Data (NSD),

Norway. Retrieved from https://doi.org/10.21338/NSD-ESS4-2008

ESS Round 5: European Social Survey Round 5 Data. (2010). Data archive and distributor of ESS data for ESS ERIC. Data file edition 3.4. Norwegian Centre for Research Data (NSD), Norway. Retrieved from https://doi.org/10.21338/NSD-ESS5-2010

ESS Round 8: European Social Survey Round 8 Data. (2016). Data archive and distributor of ESS data for ESS ERIC. Data file edition 2.1. Norwegian Centre for Research Data (NSD), Norway. Retrieved from https://doi.org/10.21338/NSD-ESS8-2016

Esser, I., & Olsen, K. M. (2012). Perceived job quality: Autonomy and job security within a multi-level framework. *European Sociological Review*, *28*(4), 443–454. doi:10.1093/esr/jcr009

Eurobarometer. (2011). Employment and social policy. Special Eurobarometer 377. Retrieved from http://ec.europa.eu/commfrontoffice/publicopinion/archives/ebs/ebs_377_en.pdf

Eurofound. (2019a). European working conditions survey 2015. Retrieved from https://www.eurofound.europa.eu/data/european-working-conditions-survey

Eurofound. (2019b). European working conditions survey 2010. Retrieved from https://www.eurofound.europa.eu/pl/data/european-working-conditions-survey-2010

Eurostat. (2019a). Employed persons expecting a possible loss of their job in the next 6 months by sex and age (source: Eurofound) [qoe_ewcs_4a5]. Retrieved from https://appsso.

eurostat.ec.europa.eu/nui/show.do?dataset=qoe_ewcs_4a5&lang=en

Eurostat. (2019b). Unemployment by sex and age-annual average [une_rt_a]. Retrieved from https://appsso.eurostat.ec.europa.eu/nui/show.do?dataset=une_rt_a&lang=en

Eurostat. (2019c). Unemployment by sex, age and duration of unemployment [lfsa_ugad]. Retrieved from https://appsso.eurostat.ec.europa.eu/nui/show.do?dataset=lfsa_ugad&lang=en

Eurostat. (2019d). Expenditure: Main results [spr_exp_sum]. Retrieved from https://appsso.eurostat.ec.europa.eu/nui/submitViewTableAction.do

Eurostat. (2019e). Mean and median income by age and sex – EU-SILC survey [ilc_di03]. Retrieved from https://appsso.eurostat.ec.europa.eu/nui/show.do?dataset=ilc_di03&lang=en

Eurostat. (2019f). Low-wage earners as a proportion of all employees (excluding apprentices) by age [earn_ses_pub1a]. Retrieved from https://appsso.eurostat.ec.europa.eu/nui/show.do?dataset=earn_ses_pub1a&lang=en

Eurostat. (2019g). Employed persons participating in job-related non-formal education and training in the past 12 months by sex and age (source: Eurofound) [qoe_ewcs_6_1]. Retrieved from https://appsso.eurostat.ec.europa.eu/nui/show.do?dataset=qoe_ewcs_6_1&lang=en

Eurostat. (2019h). Employed persons by full time/part time activity and NACE Rev. 2 activity [tour_lfs1r2]. Retrieved from https://appsso.eurostat.ec.europa.eu/nui/show.do?dataset=tour_lfs1r2&lang=en

Eurostat. (2019i). Employment in current job by duration [tepsr_wc220]. Retrieved from https://ec.europa.eu/eurostat/ tgm/table.do?tab=table&init=1&plugin=1&pcode=tepsr_ wc220&language=en

Eurostat. (2019j). Precarious employment by sex, age and NACE Rev. 2 activity [lfsa_qoe_4ax1r2]. Retrieved from https://appsso.eurostat.ec.europa.eu/nui/ submitViewTableAction.do

Eurostat. (2019k). Proportion of employees earning less than 105% of the minimum wage, October 2010 and 2014 (%). Retrieved from https://ec.europa.eu/eurostat/statistics-explained/index.php?title=File:Proportion_of_employees_ earning_less_than_105_%25_of_the_monthly_minimum_ wage,_October_2010_and_2014_(%25)_YB17_I.png& oldid=326439

Fullerton, A. S., Robertson, D. L., & Dixon, J. C. (2011). Reexamining the relationship between flexibility and insecurity: A multilevel study if perceived job insecurity in 27 European countries. In D. Brady (Ed.), *Comparing European workers Part A: Experiences and ineqaulities* (pp. 9–41). Bingley: Emerald Group Publishing.

ILO. (2013). *Decent work. Country profile Ukraine. (2nd ed.)*. Geneva: ILO.

Keune, M. (2015). Trade unions, precarious work and dualisation in Europe. In W. Eichhorst & P. Marx (Eds.), *Non-standard employment in post-industrial labour markets. An occupational perspective* (pp. 378–400). Cheltenham: Edward Elgar Publishing.

Kiersztyn, A. (2018). Non-standard employment and subjective insecurity: How can we capture job precarity using survey data? In A. L. Kalleberg & S. P. Vallas (Eds.),

Precarious work (pp. 91–122). Bingley: Emerald Publishing Limited.

Klandermans, B., Hesselink, J. K., & van Vuuren, T. (2010). Employment status and job insecurity: On the subjective appraisal of an objective status. *Economic and Industrial Democracy, 31*(4), 557–577. doi:10.1177/0143831X 09358362

Kurowska, A. (2017). Obiektywna i subiektywna sytuacja życiowa Polek i Polaków. In M. Theiss, A. Kurowska, J. Petelczyc, & B. Lewenstein (Eds.), *Obywatel na zielonej wyspie. Polityka społeczna i obywatelstwo społeczne w Polsce w dobie europejskiego kryzysu ekonomicznego* (pp. 113–150). Warszawa: Wydawnictwo Instytutu Filozofii i Socjologii PAN.

Kwiatkowski, E., & Włodarczyk, P. (2017). Znaczenie prawnej ochrony zatrudnienia. In E. Kwiatkowski (Ed.), *Instytucje rynku pracy w krajach OECD. Istota, tendencje i znaczenie ekonomiczne* (pp. 81–117). Łódź: Wydawnictwo Uniwersytetu Łódzkiego.

Marx, P. (2014). The effect of job insecurity and employability on preferences for redistribution in Western Europe. *Journal of European Social Policy, 24*(4), 351–366. doi:10.1177/0958928714538217

OECD. (2019a). The OECD indicators on employment protection legislation. Retrieved from http://www.oecd.org/employment/emp/oecdindicatorsofemploymentprotection.htm

OECD. (2019b). Active labour market policies: Connecting people with jobs. Retrieved from http://www.oecd.org/employment/activation.htm

Ogbonnaya, Ch., Gahan, P., & Eib, C. (2019). Recessionary changes at work and employee well-being: The protective roles of national and workplace institutions. *European Journal of Industrial Relations*. online first. doi:10.1177/0959680119830885

Round, J., Williams, C. C., & Rodgers, P. (2008). Corruption in the post-Soviet workplace: The experience of recent graduates in contemporary Ukraine. *Work, Employment and Society, 22*(1), 149−166. doi:10.1177/0950017007087421

SSSU. (2018). Economic activity of population in Ukraine 2017. Retrieved from https://ukrstat.org/en/druk/publicat/kat_u/2018/zb/08/EAN_2017_e.pdf

Standing, G. (2011). *The precariat. The new dangerous class.* London: Bloomsbury Academic.

WSI Minimum Wage Database. (2019). Country reports. Retrieved from https://www.boeckler.de/wsi-tarifarchiv_44071.htm

WSI Minimum Wage Database. (2019a). Minimum wages in Euro and PPS January 2018. Retrieved from https://www.boeckler.de/pdf/ta_january_2019_mwdb.pdf

CHAPTER 3

WHY AND WHERE: LABOUR MARKET SECURITY AS A PUSH-PULL FACTOR

Maciej A. Górecki, Kamil Matuszczyk and Monika Stec

INTRODUCTION

In this chapter, we analyse the impact of labour market security on contemporary Polish labour migrants' choices and perceptions, broadly conceived, of their destination countries. We adopt the 'varieties of capitalism' framework (e.g. Hall & Soskice, 2001) and argue that countries differ significantly with respect to the levels of job security their labour markets can offer. These cross-national disparities result from the broader institutional set-up of particular national economies. This theory is complementary to the theory of social models (Esping-Andersen, 1990; Golinowska, 2018), which is also discussed in this publication (see Introduction).

We exploit the fortunate fact that the two main countries of destination for labour migrants from Poland, that is, Germany and the United Kingdom, are, at the same time, considered to be 'ideal types' of, respectively, a coordinated market economy (CME) and a liberal market economy (LME). The former type offers workers substantially higher levels of job security while the latter one emphasises the 'flexibility' of employment (employment security). Using data from a survey of Polish employees in Germany and the United Kingdom as well as graduates of Polish universities who have decided to migrate to one of these two countries, we demonstrate that a tendency to prefer job security over employment security, or vice versa, has a considerable impact on Polish labour migrants' choice of a destination country. Those with a strong preference for job security tend to choose Germany with its CME, while those with a lesser preference for it, or with a preference for employment security, tend to look favourably at the United Kingdom, constituting an 'ideal type' of an LME. We supplement the aforementioned findings with data gathered in the course of 20 qualitative interviews. While the interviews add important nuance to the picture sketched earlier, they generally confirm the conjecture that preferences as regards the levels of employment security codetermine the choices of destination countries made by labour migrants. In addition, the chapter contains a brief report from seven qualitative interviews carried out with Ukrainians working in Poland. This allowed us to learn about their expectations regarding labour market security as well as to uncover differences in comparison with Polish migrants.[1]

The chapter proceeds as follows. The next section touches upon the concept of 'varieties of capitalism' as a broad conceptual framework guiding our analyses. At the end of it, we put forward hypotheses linking migrants' preferences with respect to the type of security with their choice of a destination country. The third section describes the data that we use. The fourth section presents the results of the analyses of survey data. The fifth section discusses the main findings gathered in the course of qualitative interviews. The last section summarises the chapter.

'VARIETIES OF CAPITALISM' AND EMPLOYMENT SECURITY: IMPLICATIONS FOR THE STUDY OF LABOUR MIGRATION

The theoretical framework we rely on to explain Polish migrants' choices and perceptions of the destination countries emphasises cross-national disparities as regards the institutions defining the exact functioning of particular capitalist economies. More precisely, we refer to the 'varieties of capitalism' (VoC) concept (Hall & Gingerich, 2009; Hall & Soskice, 2001). In a nutshell, the VoC theory distinguishes two 'ideal types' of organisation of capitalist economies: LMEs and CMEs. The theory of social models (see Esping-Andersen, 1990; Golinowska, 2018; Sapir, 2005) distinguishes more types of countries' socio-economic profiles, from three to five, and the boundaries between particular types are less sharp than in the case of the VoC framework.

The United Kingdom and the United States constitute 'ideal types' of LMEs, while Germany is an 'ideal type' of a CME. LMEs tend to rely heavily on the process of arm's-length exchange, regulated by the rules of free competition and formal contracting. Essentially, this type of economy is coordinated 'via hierarchies and competitive market arrangements' (Hall & Soskice, 2001, p. 8), a form of coordination depicted comprehensively by the new institutional economics literature (e.g. Williamson, 1985). CMEs are, by contrast, highly dependent on nonmarket relationships. In such an institutional context, contracting is, more often than not, incomplete and tends to be supplemented with private information shared within social networks. As such, CMEs are much more collaborative than are LMEs. While the economic outcomes in the latter ones are largely given by the respective demand and supply functions, those of the former ones emerge as a result of a 'strategic interaction' among the core participants of the given economic domain (Hall & Soskice, 2001, p. 8). In terms of the theory of social models described in Chapter 1, the United Kingdom represents the Anglo-Saxon model, while Germany represents the continental one (Sapir, 2005).

The implications stemming from the VoC framework are crucial for our understanding of the behaviour of firms and thereby also for our understanding of employment conditions characterising a given national economy. In LMEs, firms depend heavily on capital available from stock markets. In such a situation, their long-term survival requires 'flexible' institutional arrangements, facilitating instant reactions to the fluctuations of stock prices. The repercussions for labour relations are fairly obvious. In an economy such as, for example, the British one, labour markets are organised in such a way as to allow firms to easily lay off their workforce in times of lowering profitability (Hall & Soskice, 2001, p. 16). An economic environment thus emerges in which the employers prefer short-term contracts and relatively loose relationships with the employees. This implies a less tight employment protection legislation and lower levels of unionisation (Feldmann, 2006, p. 836; Hall & Soskice, 2001). The resulting levels of job security tend to be rather low. At the same time, LMEs provide all economic actors, including workers, with incentives to invest in 'switchable assets, such as general skills' (Hall & Soskice, 2001, p. 17). Thus, labour markets in LMEs tend to be more fluid and dynamic, with the relatively low job security being somewhat compensated by the apparent opportunities of switching from a declining sector of the economy to a flourishing one. Unlike with LMEs, CMEs, of which an 'ideal type' is the German economy, rely on a much more extensive set of coordination mechanisms. Stock market capitalisation is supplemented with and mediated by private information acquisition through social networks and cross-shareholding. The resulting uncertainty reduction is reinforced by relatively intense participation of the state in the economy, be it in the form of extensive regulation efforts or in a more direct manner. Moreover, deliberation between different economic actors is heavily relied on, including information exchange and bargaining between the employers and the employees (Hall & Soskice, 2001, pp. 10−12). All this creates an economic milieu with high labour union density and the prevalence of long-term contracts. Job security offered within such a context is thus relatively high.

Institutional features of a given economy that create conditions marked by high levels of job security, or a lack thereof, exert an effect on a number of relevant phenomena at the individual level. For example, subjective feelings of job insecurity tend to increase people's support for income redistribution (Marx, 2014). At the same time, these individual-level perceptions of insecurity are codetermined by the institutional arrangements discussed above. While the VoC approach, with its fundamental distinction between LMEs and CMEs, may tell only a part of the story explaining people's subjectively perceived labour market security, this part of the story is certainly non-negligible. For instance, labour union density is a very robust predictor having a substantial negative effect on subjective job insecurity (e.g. Dixon, Fullerton, & Robertson, 2013). Furthermore, analyses comparing self-perceived job insecurity levels between permanent workers and those on temporary contracts, that is, those whose feelings of insecurity should be by definition higher, indicated that the perceived insecurity gap between those two groups widened in the countries with more extensive job protection regulations. Apparently, the lack of such regulations creates conditions under which self-perceived job situation of permanent workers is less easily distinguishable from that of temporary ones (e.g. Balz, 2017). In other words, in the 'flexible' LMEs, substantial numbers of workers feel insecure regardless of a type of contract, while in CMEs the divergence between permanent and temporary workers is more pronounced. Last but not least, structural conditions affecting the quality of employment, including job insecurity, tend to have an impact on labour migrants' subjective well-being. In particular, according to the concept of 'social anchoring' (Grzymała-Kazłowska, 2018), 'precarious' employment conditions, such as short-term or zero-hour contracts, might have broader negative consequences for migrants' ability to 'settle emotionally' in the new place and integrate with the receiving society to a sufficient degree. Summarising, there seems to be plenty of evidence suggesting that the institutional features of a given economy (type of capitalism) exert a strong effect on the way individuals cope with their daily lives.

In this chapter, we put forward a proposition that links labour migrants' preferences regarding labour market security (preference job vs employment security) with their choice of a destination country. We study choices made Polish migrants and exploit the fact that the destinations they choose most often are Germany and the United Kingdom. The former is considered an 'ideal type' of a CME and the latter an 'ideal type' of an LME. In claiming so, we follow in the footsteps of Hall and Soskice (2001, pp. 18–21) who make a clear-cut distinction between the national economies whose crucial institutions are predominantly of an LME type and those whose institutional set-up is predominantly of a CME type. Both groups of national economies can be considered reasonably 'institutionally coherent' (see Kenworthy, 2006).

The LME countries group is comprised of the United Kingdom, the United States, Australia, Canada, New Zealand and Ireland, while Germany, Japan, Switzerland, the Netherlands, Belgium, Sweden, Norway, Denmark, Finland and Austria are classified as CMEs. Other advanced industrial economies (e.g. France) display a considerable degree of 'ambiguity' as regards economic institutions (Hall & Soskice, 2001, p. 21). Anyway, Germany and the United Kingdom leave no doubt as to their being, respectively, a CME and an LME. We thus propose the following main hypotheses which will drive the empirical analyses that follow.

> *H1.* Preferences for job security (over employment) will tend to increase Polish labour migrants' propensity to choose Germany, that is, a CME, as a destination country.
>
> *H2.* Preferences for employment security (over job security) will tend to increase Polish labour migrants' propensity to choose the United Kingdom, that is, an LME, as a destination country.

DATA AND CONCEPT OF ANALYSIS

The empirical analysis we conduct comprises two parts. In the first part, we use survey data in order to quantitatively test the two aforementioned hypotheses. A survey questionnaire was administered to a sample of 200 respondents. Half of those were Polish labour migrants employed and living in either Germany or the United Kingdom. The other half was comprised of graduates of Polish universities who declared that they had decided to permanently emigrate from Poland in search of better employment opportunities. Fifty-five of those pointed to either Germany or the United Kingdom as a destination country. There were missing data problems concerning one of those respondents which left us with 154 observations available for an analysis of the determinants of migrants' choice between Germany and the United Kingdom. At the same time, we notice the fact that some of the university graduates surveyed mentioned countries that, according to what was said in the previous section, can be unambiguously classified as either CMEs (e.g. Norway, Sweden) or LMEs (e.g. the United States, Canada, Australia). As a robustness check, we thus analyse a broader set of respondents choosing between CMEs and LMEs. A total of 185 observations are available for such an extended analysis. The dependent variable we set out to explain is a binary one taking the value of one in case a respondent chose Germany (a CME in the case of the extended analysis) as a destination country of labour migration and the value of zero in case a respondent chose the United Kingdom (an LME in the case of the extended analysis).

Our core explanatory variable is what we call 'Preference for type of security'. During the interview, respondents were asked, among other things, to explain what they mean by 'feeling secure in a labour market'. Thirteen answers/statements were presented to them out of which they were asked to select four they agreed most in the context of the issue of job security. The statements were the following:

(1) I have a job protected by the law, so it would be hard to lay me off.

(2) In case of losing a job, I can count on help on part of various institutions, such as labour unions or employment offices.

(3) If I work I can receive various benefits, be it for children or for a non-working spouse.

(4) I am sure that if I lose a job then I will find another one without any trouble.

(5) I have signed an employment contract.

(6) The state supports those who work (e.g. by offering them various 'bonuses') rather than those who are unemployed (e.g. by offering them unemployment benefits).

(7) The state offers generous unemployment benefits to allow the unemployed for seeking an appropriate employment rather than accepting any one that becomes available.

(8) The state guarantees high minimum wages so that one's income fully covers the costs of one's existence.

(9) It is better to work more and earn a higher salary instead of counting on various state-funded benefits.

(10) It is better to have opportunities of switching jobs often (I may lose a job, but I can quickly find another one) rather than fighting with an employer not to lose a job at any cost (e.g. take an employer to a court or report an employer to labour unions).

(11) The state always takes sides with an employee, helping him/her in the event of a conflict with an employer.

(12) The state cares for workers' achieving balance between work and family life.

(13) Language proficiency makes me feel secure as regards employment.

Out of the above 13 statements, we classified the following eight ones as emphasising 'security' and thus being likely chosen by those who prefer labour market arrangements characteristic of CMEs: 1, 2, 3, 5, 7, 8, 11 and 12. These statements emphasise either employment protection and job permanency (statements 1 and 5), or the need for help from the state for the unemployed (statements 2 and 3), or the necessity of other types of state intervention in the labour market, including generous employment benefits and minimum wages (statements 7, 8, 11 and 12). The other five statements refer to either an employee's self-sufficiency and ability to cope with one's situation successfully after losing a job (statements 4 and 10), or the necessity of limiting state-funded 'bonuses' to those already in employment only (statement 6), or particular 'helpful' individual qualities, such as the ability to work hard and language skills (statements 9 and 13). We thus expect that the respondents choosing those statements will look favourably at the LMEs and labour markets typical for this type of capitalist economies. Having classified the statements as favouring either 'job security' or 'employment security', we calculate our main explanatory variable, that is, an index showing what proportion of the four statements selected by a particular respondent are ones emphasising 'job security'.

Apart from the aforementioned core independent variable, the models we estimate include a few control variables. Given the rather modest number of observations available for an analysis, we limit the number of controls. We control for a respondent's gender, natural logarithm of age (in years), a binary variable indicating whether or not a respondent has children under the age of 18 living at home, and a dummy variable distinguishing between the two subsamples (graduates vs employees). In addition, we include interactions of the subsample dummy with the logarithm of age and with the main explanatory variable, that is, the aforementioned 'preference for job security' index. As our dependent variable is a binary one, we rely on probit regression to estimate the effects of the variables of interest on migrants' choice of a destination country. We estimate the particular effects of interest using CLARIFY software (King, Tomz, & Wittenberg, 2000).

A separate part of this chapter is constituted by an analysis of data collected in the course of 27 qualitative (in-depth) interviews. Ten of our interviewees were Polish migrants employed in either Germany or the United Kingdom, five persons in each country. Two of those living and working in Germany and four of those from the United Kingdom were women. The youngest interviewee was 28 and the oldest was one 66 at the time of the interview. At the same time, six of them, that is, a majority, were in their 30s. Also, 10 graduates from Polish universities having decided to emigrate from Poland were interviewed. Seven of those were women. All of these interviewees were in their 20s, the youngest and the oldest being 22 and 26, respectively. Out of the 10 graduates interviewed, four declared that they had decided to emigrate to the United Kingdom or the United States, that is, LMEs. Three persons indicated they would go to Germany or Sweden, that is, CMEs. The three remaining interviewees were either undecided (one person) or had decided to move to France, that is, a country with 'ambiguous' economic institutions (see Hall & Soskice, 2001; Kenworthy, 2006). The third group of interviewees analysed separately, comprised Ukrainian immigrants who have been employed in Poland for at least 12 months. The sample included two women and five men, in the age bracket 25–45 years.

We analyse the transcripts of the interviews described here in order to deepen our understanding of the impact of labour market institutions, and broader organisation of particular national economies, on labour migrants' decisions of which of the available destinations to choose. To make it possible, a number of issues related to respondents' preferences as regards labour market institutions were touched upon in this qualitative part of our study.

MIGRANTS' CHOICE OF DESTINATION COUNTRY: SURVEY DATA ANALYSIS

Probit regression estimates for models that aim to explain Polish labour migrants' choice of a destination country are presented in Table 1. Positive effects of the variable 'Preference for job security' indicate that, all else being equal, the more a respondent values job security the more likely she is to choose Germany or, more generally, a CME. Our hypotheses thus seem to be corroborated. Importantly, both crucial effects are statistically significant at conventional levels, respective p-values falling below 0.01 and 0.05 for the restricted model and the extended one, respectively.

Although, at first look, the results seem to confirm our hypotheses, it must be remembered that inferences from non-linear models, such as probit, drawn solely on the basis of regression coefficients, might be misleading (see e.g. Ai & Norton, 2003). We thus estimated marginal effects of an increase in the index of 'Preference for job security' from its minimum to median value on the probability of a respondent choosing Germany (CME) as a destination country. Figure 1 below presents those effects graphically.

Figure 1 shows that marginal effects of an increase in the 'Preference for job security' index are very strong. For example, if the index rises from its minimum (0) to median (0.75) value the probability of a university graduate choosing Germany rather than the United Kingdom as a destination

Table 1. Predictors of Polish Labour Migrants' Choice of Destination Country: Probit Regression Estimates.

	Germany vs UK	CME vs LME
Preference for job security	3.90**	1.86*
	(1.25)	(0.86)
Female	0.14	−0.01
	(0.22)	(0.19)
Ln(Age)	−4.07	−1.90
	(3.58)	(2.12)
Has children under age of 18	−0.19	−0.22
	(0.24)	(0.23)
Employee	−9.95	−4.46
	(11.49)	(7.05)
Employee × Preference for job security	−2.38*	−0.34
	(1.39)	(1.07)
Employee × Ln(Age)	3.74	1.55
	(3.60)	(2.17)
Constant	10.19	4.90
	(11.39)	(6.84)
LL	−93.86	−120.50
McFadden R^2	0.12	0.06
N	154	185

Note: $*p < 0.05$; $**p < 0.01$. Main entries are unstandardised regression coefficients and the numbers in round brackets are robust standard errors.

country increases by approximately 33.5 percentage points (see left panel). The corresponding effect for Polish migrants already working and living abroad (employees) is even slightly stronger, an increase by about 38.4 percentage

Figure 1. Effects of Job Security Preference on Polish Migrants' Choice of Destination Country.

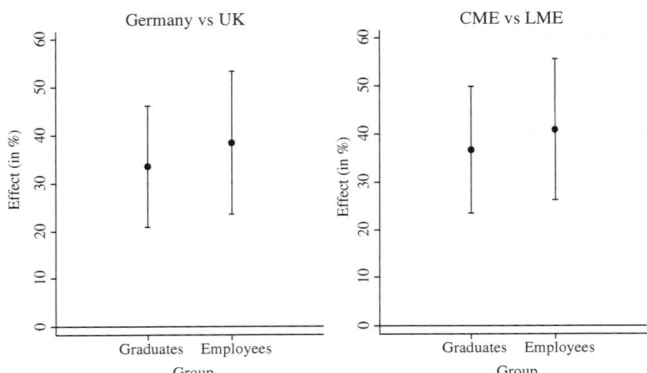

Notes: Effects of an increase in job security preference from its minimum to median value are plotted. Control variables are held at their medians. Vertical bars represent 95% CIs.

points. The effects for a more general choice between a CME and an LME are comparable and thus reassuring. It is so especially as none of the 95 % confidence intervals accompanying the plotted effects encompasses zero, which again confirms that the results are statistically significant at conventional levels. The remarkable similarities between the analyses for different response variables, as well as between the two groups of respondents, indicate that the evidence supporting our main hypotheses is robust. At the same time, we notice that the control variables we included in our models do not seem to have a statistically significant impact on the migrants' choice of a destination country. Arguably, there does also seem to be a substantial random variation as regards the aforementioned choice or, at the very least, a substantial part of variation unaccounted for by our models. All in all, however Polish labour migrants' preferences with respect to types of labour market security offered by respective national economies appear to be an important factor driving their decisions of where, eventually, to move and settle.

MIGRANTS' CHOICE OF DESTINATION COUNTRIES: IN-DEPTH INTERVIEWS

The outcome of the individual in-depth interviews carried out among emigrants and among graduates of Polish universities who have decided to emigrate has largely confirmed our conclusions drawn so far. The principal motivation of both pursuing and planning migration is related to earnings. Emigration means, first and foremost, a chance to improve one's financial situation and, second, opportunities for professional development.

In our interviewees' view, incomes, substantially higher relative to those available in their country of origin, are expected to contribute to their reaching income security. This would allow for gaining labour market security and accumulating financial resources necessary for maintaining security in case of transient unemployment. One of the interviewees describes the relationship between income security and labour market security as follows:

> *It seems that finances and security go hand in hand [...]. This is also the element of security, that means you earn enough to support yourself and to have some kind of monetary shield in case you were laid off, or if you broke your back and required medical treatment. Thus, salary contributes to labour market security. (Graduate, Warsaw – Female, 25 years)*

At the same time, the interviewees differ somewhat as regards their expectations of gaining income security and labour market security. Those living in Germany or planning to go to that country tend to pay a great deal of attention to the elements comprising the concept of job security. Work in Germany is stable and workers performing their duties conscientiously and diligently need not be afraid of losing their jobs. This characteristic of their employment situation is valued very highly by our interviewees. Moreover, in view of those with long-term experience of the German labour market, labour relations in Germany meet extremely high standards. One of such interviewees, having worked in Germany for several years, describes his experience as follows:

> *I felt no anxiety that I would lose that job. There are no excessive demands like that [...] from employers. If you prove yourself a good worker, they let you develop; they don't press you that much. (Worker, Germany – Male, 34 years)*

Having an employment contract signed, is of great importance for the workers employed in Germany. Owing to it, they could achieve labour market security. It is illustrated well by the following statements:

> *In Germany, everybody works under a labour code contracts and has all the benefits. (Worker, Germany – Male, 28 years)*

> *The essential contract that you get is the labour code contract. In no way can you be employed in differently, and that's what I like. Somehow, that market simply functions this way. (Worker, Germany – Male, 33 years)*

Workers deciding to undertake employment in Germany can count on a high level of social security, strengthened by permanent employment status that guarantees them numerous benefits. The relatively high quality of employment in Germany, pointed out by migrants, is guaranteed through, among others, stable work arrangements and an extensive network of labour market institutions. In the interviewees' narratives, there repeatedly appear references to the German labour market as providing stabilisation, security and comfort. Obviously, it is not social benefits alone, despite their being very generous in Germany, that attract workers from Poland. Nevertheless, the mere awareness that in the case of unemployment or any other financial trouble one can take advantage of them gives one the sense of income security. This translates into the perspective of 'normal life'. It is suggestively illustrated by the following excerpt from one of the interviews:

> *Everything protects you, because you are working. [...] It is not so, that today [the employer] lays you off and from tomorrow he doesn't pay you, there is a period of notice [...]. He must have a really solid grounds, otherwise it cannot pay for him [...] Here the labour law is very good. (Worker, Germany – Male, 28 years)*

The interviewees employed in the United Kingdom and the university graduates planning to go there are more likely than those choosing Germany to mention the relative ease of finding employment, preferably quickly. This applies to both the first employment and the subsequent ones. According to their views, the British labour market offers such a great number of different job offers that finding employment presents no problem. This means that, in their opinion, labour market security can be achieved through employment security. One of the respondents put it as follows:

> *Job offers, here there is plenty of work. It is not so that anyone has no job. There are jobs. I think that those who say there is no work, they are those who don't feel like working. (Worker, the UK — Male, 35 years)*

Largely similar views were expressed by graduates intending to emigrate from Poland. In their opinions, the decision to migrate to the United Kingdom rather than elsewhere was influenced by the possibility of finding satisfactory employment and by the ease of job switching if necessary. One of them noted the high supply of jobs:

> *If you cannot find a job within three days, it must mean you don't want to look for a job at all. It is simply very easy to find a job, very easy to find a school, or, in general, many world-wide companies like that have their branches there. (Graduate, Rzeszów — Male, 22 years)*

Similarly to those settling in Germany, the migrants from Poland in the United Kingdom appreciate the conditions of employment in the British labour market. They emphasise the level of salaries that secures them a normal decent life:

> *Whereas the advantage of working in the United Kingdom is, of course, the salary, which is decent and you can manage to live on it. (Graduate, Warsaw — Female, 25 years)*

To summarise, for all groups of interviewees, it is earnings that is the most important motivation or justification for going abroad. Labour market security tends to be seen by them through the prism of income. Other dimensions related directly to labour market appear to be less important for making migration-related decisions. At the same time, the statements quoted above demonstrate noticeable heterogeneity with respect to the exact ways in which labour market security is reached. In the German labour market, security is provided based on instruments comprising the construct of job security, while the British labour market promotes employment security. Nonetheless, it is worth emphasising that our interviewees view both the German and British labour market as in all respects superior to the Polish one.

As mentioned in the introduction to this chapter, Ukrainians working in Poland were interviewed in the course of the research project as well. As in the case of Poles, their most important motivation for emigration is higher earnings, that is, income security. The disparity in earnings between Poland and Ukraine is very pronounced. The wages obtained in Poland are high enough to cover the maintenance costs and, in addition, accumulate savings to be sent to families in Ukraine. At the same time, the Ukrainians pointed to the relevance of the factors pushing them out of their country. According to their narratives, the Ukrainian labour legislation does not meet standards abided by in the European Union. Existing regulations are faulty, and even these are bypassed by employers. That is why Ukrainians attach great value to the labour market security they can obtain in Poland.

> *Here I am not bothered about the future, I am fine, if I pay taxes, I can keep calm, I pay for health insurance, for a pension, for everything, insurance in case of accident and for disability pension. For me that peace gives me the possibility to build something. In our country, in Ukraine, there is*

> *nothing like that, you live one day at a time, you do not know what tomorrow will bring, maybe you will not be able to afford bread. (Ukrainian, Warsaw – Female, 45 years)*

Pervasive corruption is a crucial factor determining decisions to emigrate from Ukraine. It was emphasised by all the persons interviewed. Getting a job which would allow for achieving income security is often preceded by the necessity of bribing someone. Even that, however, is no guarantee that the job will be maintained in the long run. The situation in Poland in this respect is much better. This is how one of the interviewees compared the two countries:

> *My point is that in Poland there are more opportunities, compared to Ukraine, much more chances, much more feeling that nobody will exploit you, that you will not be thrown on the street only because someone else paid more for the job you have. (Ukrainian, Warsaw – Male, 26 years)*

Labour market security in Poland is evaluated much higher than that in Ukraine. In spite of that, however, the prevalent opinion of the Ukrainians is that they tend not to achieve an entirely satisfactory living standard in Poland. At the same time, they are aware that the more experience they have, the easier it will be for them to find their way in the labour market, especially when they happen to lose a job. This is how one of the respondents described the issue of security in the Polish labour market,

> *I do not feel secure because I know it is a job which will come to an end sooner or later. I know that I will get my wages till the end of this year, as it is in the budget. Whereas, regarding further employment*

> *I will have to look for a more stable and secure place. Now I am working in order to gain experience which I will be able to show at my next job interview and while looking for the next employment. And then I will aim for a work with an employment contract, this is a result of my plans for the future, as I am seriously considering buying a flat in Poland.*
> *(Ukrainian, Warsaw — Male, 24 years)*

It follows from the above statement and from similar ones made by other interviewees that the views of the Ukrainians depend on how long they have been staying in Poland. At the beginning of their stay, they tend to prefer employment security, as this is perhaps the way in which they can obtain a higher level of income security. They work harder and longer hours than Poles, sometimes for more than one employer, and they keep their leisure time to a minimum. As time passes, they start doing their best to find permanent employment and then their views gradually evolve toward preferring job security. In the case of migrants from Ukraine, it is the geographical proximity to Poland that also matters a lot. It follows from their narratives that they appreciate the fact that, in case they lose a job and cannot find another one, they can easily and quickly return to their country of origin. This is a sort of safety valve for them, a strategy which allows for increasing the level of their labour market security.

All in all, the factors pushing migrants from Ukraine to Poland differ to a certain degree from those characteristic of Polish migrants. For Ukrainians, in addition to low earnings, corruption constitutes a factor that puts serious obstacles on their way to reaching income security. The Polish labour market is perceived by them as superior to that in Ukraine, albeit the level of labour market security it offers is still considered suboptimal. For the Ukrainians in Poland, income security is much more likely to be reached through employment security. If they have experience in the work they perform, they have no problems changing employment. However, we should be aware of the restrictions resulting from the fact that, as the third-country citizens, they are obliged to get various kinds of labour permits and residence permits. This makes reaching labour market security through job security rather hard, especially as their jobs are often short-term only.

CONCLUSIONS

The analyses presented in this chapter largely confirm the hypotheses we put forward. Labour market security is certainly a significant factor taken into consideration by all the migrants interviewed. However, particular categories of our respondents and interviewees differ with respect to their preferred type of labour market security. Some of them choose countries where they can accomplish that security through job security, while others find their way better in countries where the model based on employment security is favoured. The former category tends to choose Germany, while the latter tends to prefer the United Kingdom, at least as long as Polish emigrants are considered. Ukrainians coming to Poland are more likely to arrive at the state of labour market security through employment security. However, their access to employment contracts is severely limited and this diminishes the probability of their pursuing the strategy of job security. Thus, their 'choice' is, more often than not, an involuntary way of adapting to circumstances. Last but not least, there is yet another very important aspect on which the perspective of Poles employed either in Germany or in the United Kingdom differs considerably from that of Ukrainians in Poland. While the latter's priorities are the stability of earnings and the relative freedom from corruption, Polish migrants emphasise the 'normal life' they can live as a result of working in other EU member states.

NOTE

1. Both the qualitative and quantitative research was carried out by the research firm DANAE. All respondents gave their consent to use their statements anonymously in scholarly publications presenting the results of the research project.

REFERENCES

Ai, Ch., & Norton, E. C. (2003). Interaction terms in logit and probit models. *Economics Letters*, *80*(1), 123–129. doi:10.1016/S0165-1765(03)00032-6.

Balz, A. (2017). Cross-national variations in the security gap: Perceived job insecurity among temporary and permanent employees and employment protection legislation. *European Sociological Review*, *33*(5), 675–692. doi:10.1093/esr/jcx067.

Dixon, J. C., Fullerton, A. S., & Robertson, D. L. (2013). Cross-national differences in workers' perceived job, labour market, and employment insecurity in Europe: Empirical tests and theoretical extensions. *European Sociological Review*, *29*(5), 1053–1067. doi:10.1093/esr/jcs084.

Esping-Andersen, G. (1990). *The three worlds of welfare capitalism*. Cambridge: Polity Press.

Feldmann, M. (2006). Emerging varieties of capitalism in transition countries: Industrial relations and wage bargaining in Estonia and Slovenia. *Comparative Political Studies*, *39*(7), 829–854. doi:10.1177/0010414006288261.

Golinowska, S. (2018). *Modele polityki społecznej w Polsce i Europie na początku XXI wieku*. Warszawa: Fundacja Batorego.

Grzymała-Kazłowska, A. (2018). From connecting to social anchoring: Adaptation and 'settlement' of Polish migrants in the UK. *Journal of Ethnic and Migration Studies*, *44*(2), 252–269. doi:10.1080/1369183X.2017.1341713.

Hall, P. A., & Gingerich, D. W. (2009). Varieties of capitalism and institutional complementarities in the political economy: An empirical analysis. *British Journal of Political Science*, *39*(3), 449–482. doi:10.1017/S0007123409000672.

Hall, P. A., & Soskice, D. (2001). *Varieties of capitalism: The institutional foundations of comparative advantage*. Oxford: Oxford University Press.

Kenworthy, L. (2006). Institutional coherence and macroeconomic performance. *Socio-Economic Review*, *4*(1), 69–91. doi:10.1093/SER/mwj032.

King, G., Tomz, M., & Wittenberg, J. (2000). *Making the most of statistical analyses: Improving interpretation and presentation*. Retrieved from https://s3.amazonaws.com/academia.edu.documents/30660604/king98f.pdf?AWSAccessKeyId=AKIAIWOWYYGZ2Y53UL3A&Expires=1559405761&Signature=z%2FDkEzLhT9oxjGFSscJiXKioMm4%3D&response-content-disposition=inline%3B%20filename%3DMaking_the_most_of_statistical_analyses.pdf.

Marx, P. (2014). The effect of job insecurity and employability on preferences for redistribution in Western Europe. *Journal of European Social Policy*, 24(4), 351–366. doi:10.1177/0958928714538217.

Sapir, A. (2005). Globalisation and the reform of European social model. *Bruegel*. Retrieved from http://bruegel.org/wp-content/uploads/imported/publications/pc_sept2005_socialmod.pdf

Williamson, O. E. (1985). Reflections on the new institutional economics. *Zeitschrift für die gesamte Staatswissenschaft*, 141, 187–195.

CHAPTER 4

MIGRATION POLICY: RECOMMENDATIONS FOR SENDING AND RECEIVING COUNTRIES

Maciej Duszczyk

Making migration-related decisions involves complex multidimensional considerations, not least because the consequences of such decisions extend also to members of one's households. From the meso- and macro-level perspectives, migration decisions made by individuals have an impact on their respective local communities and even entire countries, both the sending and the receiving ones. Immigrants' choice of a given country or region brings about change to its economic and social profile. In recent years, migrations have also become an important political issue, constituting the main issue of numerous election campaigns and political disputes. For example, the already mentioned influx of great numbers of immigrants to the United Kingdom, a result largely of the free movement of workers within the European Union (EU), became one of the driving forces of the successful Brexit campaign. Of course, there are more countries where debates on immigration and the immigrant' status have taken place in recent years. We can certainly say that there is no country in the EU where the issue of immigration would not constitute a fundamental political cleavage line. As a result of such political debates, immigration policies have been tightened. Likewise, the scope of benefits offered to immigrants has been limited in an attempt to limit social advantages resulting from migration. Thus, the pull factor, emphasised by the 'welfare' magnet hypothesis mentioned in the introduction and the first chapter of this publication, has waned. This new situation means a necessity of recognising and understanding the motivations of individual (micro-level) migration-related decisions. Such an in-depth knowledge would facilitate the management of migration processes on part of both sending countries and the receiving ones. We assume that the sending countries will still face a situation in which both stimulating and limiting emigration is a conceivable strategy. Their choice of particular strategies will depend on, among other things, their demographic situation, the unemployment rate, the phase of economic transformation and the need for supporting households with financial resources coming from abroad. The conditions faced by the receiving countries are complex and dynamic as well. There will be periods when a liberal migration policy would be advisable while other times would favour restrictive migration policy alternatives. Furthermore, it is possible to stimulate an influx of particular categories of migrants, based on, for example, qualification levels or strictly defined expertise. We should also take into consideration the fact that, more often than not, the interests of sending and receiving countries will be divergent or even conflicting. For example, the sending countries may accuse the receiving ones of selectively attracting persons with unique qualifications, which would cause a shortage of certain experts in a sending country. This applies, for instance, to the migration of scholars or doctors of medicine. To summarise, both the sending and the receiving countries should choose migration policies adequate to their specificity. However, neither policy programming nor its implementation will be feasible without detailed knowledge of the factors determining migrants' decisions. The 'push and pull' theory is helpful here because it assembles and combines a variety of factors taken into consideration when one makes a decision to migrate and eventually chooses a destination country.

In the present publication, we have focused on labour market security, a factor so far largely neglected by those analysing migrants' decisions. While most of the classic publications on the topic argue that it is cross-country differences in earnings that are the crucial migration factor, we should not ignore other factors potentially taken into consideration by migrants. Their significance increases as the wage differences between countries begin to dwindle. Apart from the mere access to the attractively remunerated job offers, it is also the quality of work, broadly conceived, that may matter a great deal for persons deciding to emigrate. The quality of work is a multi-dimensional construct of which labour market security is certainly a crucial element.

The results of the empirical research presented in this publication have demonstrated that labour market security matters for both the decision on whether or not to migrate and the choice of a destination country. Migrants decide to leave their home country in order to secure a decent and stable income and their decision on where to emigrate depends largely on their preferences with respect to the exact mode in which income security is reached and maintained. This means migration policy-makers should perhaps include labour market security in a set of migration-relevant factors when designing instruments encouraging or discouraging particular categories of migrants.

The term 'migration policy' is conceived of broadly in this publication. For the receiving countries, it is *the set of provisions and other legal instruments regulating relationships between a given country and foreigners willing to come or stay in its territory* (Hollifield, 1992, pp. 19–44) or, even more broadly, it is

> *the conscious activity of a state aiming at achieving optimal scale and structure of the influx of foreigners, who would increase the economic competitiveness of that state without giving rise to social strains at the same time (Duszczyk, 2012, pp. 39–40)*

The above definition can be easily adapted to the specificity of the sending countries. In accordance with this approach, migration policy implemented by the sending countries would mean *conscious activities of a state aimed at achieving optimal scale and structure of the outflow of its citizens without limiting the opportunities of the country's development.* It is aimed at economic profits, among other things, in the form of inflow of financial resources as well as solving demographic problems without negative or even limited negative effects on social cohesion. Migration policies defined in this manner, including levels of labour market security offered and models of reaching it will, depending on the perspective taken, constitute either push or pull factors.

CONCLUSIONS AND RECOMMENDATIONS FOR SENDING AND RECEIVING COUNTRIES

The results of our analyses, primarily those included in Chapter 3, show that labour market security, understood as income security, can be reached in two different ways, namely through either job security or employment security. Migrants will choose different countries depending on their own expectations and their preferred model of reaching labour market security. Those oriented towards stabilisation, risk-averse and uninterested in frequent changes of employers will tend to choose countries implementing the job security model. Germany is an ideal-type example of such a country. The risk-accepting people, confident in their own expertise and inclined to change employers often in search of better employment conditions, will tend to choose countries that favour the employment security model. The United Kingdom serves as a classic example of such a model. In addition to Germany and the United Kingdom, our analyses have also focused on countries undergoing the processes of socio-economic transformation, namely Poland and Ukraine. Poland is a country of both emigration and immigration, with both processes being of a high magnitude. In other words, it is simultaneously a sending country and a receiving one. It is thus a case for which labour market security issues are fairly peculiar and, as such, difficult to interpret. Ukraine, on the contrary, is a country of purely emigration (sending country), struggling with severe economic and political conditions. Reaching the state of labour market security in that country is an enormous challenge and it seems that without addressing this issue comprehensively by the country's social and economic policy, limiting the scale of emigration substantially will be impossible.

Conclusions following from the sources obtained in the course of our research allow for suggesting the following recommendations for the sending and receiving countries:

Sending Countries

Democracies implementing free market economic principles are unable to pursue migration policies legally disallowing their citizens to settle abroad. The right to leave a country is one of the basic human rights. The only exception applies to persons who have that right suspended because of their being suspect of committing a crime. Of course, the situation is different under authoritarian regimes that may limit citizens' access to passports. No such country was subject to an analysis in the course of our research project. Nevertheless, migration policies may resort to an application of other economic or social measures in an attempt to stop or reduce emigration flows. In other words, even democratic sending countries can, to an extent, both stimulate the migration of their citizens and discourage them from migrating. As long as the issues of labour market security are considered, the following catalogue of moves can be imagined:

- A sending country implements regulations in the sphere of labour legislation which would influence migration-related decisions. If a country is interested in migration of certain categories of citizens then legal instruments should contribute to limiting their labour market security. An example, introducing regulations which would reduce the previous level of job security towards greater flexibility can stimulate emigration of those categories of citizens who value the stability of employment. (The conceivable solutions could include, for example shortening of the notice period, or limiting allowances resulting from employment in a particular sector, thereby affecting incomes, or extending working time.) Facing a change of employment, such workers may consider going abroad as an alternative to looking for another job in their country of origin. When it comes to persons whom the country wishes to stop from emigrating, an increase of job security would be worth considering. Reaching the state of stability in the work they perform would limit their propensity to emigrate. Such persons would be anxious about losing employment without being convinced that they will find another one, comparable or better, in the near future, be it in their home country or abroad. At the same time, an implementation of labour regulations would be received negatively by people with a tendency to change employers often, confident in their own skills and being able to find their way in the labour market. Greater rigidity of labour legislation could lead to an increase in emigration of people who are convinced that frequent job switching in pursuit for optimal employment is advantageous for them. In case there are no such possibilities in the country of origin, they would decide to emigrate in order not to be bound to a single employer for a long time. This means that each decision in the domain of labour legislation should be analysed in terms of migration-related consequences.

- The next move could involve a well-developed range of offers of professional training and re-training for those ready to change employment and thus aiming for an increase in their own employability. A country interested in reducing emigration should have a rich menu of offers of training directed at an improvement of qualifications or, at the very least, maintaining professional activity. Such opportunities should be available to both the unemployed and those who change employment. In practice, such training opportunities can be organised by a wide range of actors, including public institutions, trade unions, organisations of employers and NGOs. The last ones, in particular, tend to have the ability to adapt quickly to changing circumstances. Nonetheless, securing for them steady financing from public sources is of key importance. Otherwise, persons who are short-time unemployed or voluntarily changing employment may find themselves in a situation in which they are left to themselves. This would increase their propensity to emigrate in search for restoring their lost labour market security. States that aim to stimulate emigration should, on the contrary, reduce all forms of active support for the short-time unemployed in order to indirectly stimulate their leaving of the country of origin.

- Yet another step that could be undertaken is that of economic support in the form of social transfers for the unemployed and for people switching jobs voluntarily, albeit this could be implemented only to a limited extent. It should be assumed that the vast majority of sending countries have very limited funds they could spend on direct economic support for those who would otherwise emigrate. If, nevertheless, there are adequate resources in the state budget, both the short-time unemployed persons and those who are willing to change employment should be receiving state-funded support for a certain period of time. Examples relevant here are benefits offered solely to those who are actively looking for a job, or covering the costs of training courses aimed at improving the beneficiaries' professional qualifications. Raising the amount of tax-free allowance is another way to support people facing a deficit of labour market security. Employed persons earning low wages could receive a tax refund and that would increase their income security. Other social transfers, such as family benefits, can also be relied on. An example is the Polish programme named 500+. It provides financial support to families with children and, as such, has the potential of diminishing the magnitude of emigration simply because it can enhance income security. In applying this type of instruments, achieving a kind of balance is necessary between offering people labour market security, on the one hand, and, on the other, maintaining their readiness to undertake new employment.

It is also possible to programme the system in such way as to prioritise supporting the groups whose emigration the state wishes to prevent. For example, the amount of benefits could be related to employment tenure or level of education.

To summarise, although democracies cannot limit emigration by means of a direct legal ban, they are able to impact the flow of departures through measures either increasing or reducing labour market security. Instruments from the domain of labour law and social security are of special importance. Various kinds of instruments can be designed in such way as to stimulate migration-related decisions or prevent certain categories of citizens from making such decisions.

Receiving Countries

Unlike the sending countries, the receiving ones are in a position to apply a plethora of legal provisions in the migration policy domain. Such provisions can either attract foreigners or discourage them from coming and settling in a respective country. The most common means of this sort is visa policies. In principle, visas are issued only to those whose entry and stay in a given country is seen as advantageous for that country. EU member states restrict their sovereignty in this respect by implementing a common visa policy directed at third-country citizens.

At the same time, EU member states can apply certain types of instruments either stimulating or restraining immigration into their territories of migrants from both within the EU and from third countries. We can point out the following instruments that focus on the issues of labour market security and, at the same time, affect migration-related decisions:

- Results of the analyses presented in Chapter 3 indicate that the predominant model of reaching labour market security has an impact on which categories of immigrants a given country will tend to attract. Thus, countries interested in an inflow of foreigners inclined to switch jobs often as well as those with qualifications sought after by employers from the top segment of the labour market should favour flexible forms of employment, that is, employment security.

    At the same time, the aforementioned countries should be aware of the risk involved when relying on such solutions. Once the situation in their labour markets deteriorates, persons in possession of marketable qualifications and skills will quickly decide to leave the country and look for a more attractive labour market. In principle, these are highly mobile persons, especially the youngest of them. A situation of an 'exodus' of such people can now be observed in the United Kingdom, facing the prospects of Brexit. Accordingly, a recent report by the Institute of Directors, quoted by *The Guardian*, shows that one-third of the firms currently operating in the United Kingdom are planning to relocate their activities to other countries (*The Guardian*, 2019). However, countries interested in an influx of workers who tend to look for more stability and are not inclined to switch employers frequently should rather favour the model based on the stability of employment, that is, job security. Competition for employees is growing, especially in the context of aging societies and the associated decline in labour supply. Offers of stable employment are thus likely to occur more and more often. Companies confident in their own capabilities of long-term survival may consider guaranteeing stability for those employees who are of key importance for their functioning. They will do so, fearing that valuable workers can be taken over by their competitors, often ones from abroad.

Thus, regulations in the area of labour relations, adopted by a respective state, should support entrepreneurs in their applying of the aforementioned solutions. Undoubtedly, it is the role of the state to create regulations responding to the needs of employers. However, it should be noted that countries choosing solutions based on job security also take risks when implementing them, even if the risks differ from those faced by countries favouring the model of employment security. Once a foreigner has received a stable employment contract, he/she will be prone to remain in the receiving country. In the event that the situation in the labour market deteriorates, it would be rather difficult to persuade him/her to return to his/her country of origin or look for employment elsewhere. In this case, the menu of measures limiting the share of foreigners in the particular labour market is not as extensive as in the case of states where the model of employment security prevails. It should be assumed, however, that countries preferring job security find it easier to pursue a policy of integration. Immigrants enjoying stable employment conditions are likely to integrate with the dominant ethnic group in the society. A related dilemma is currently being faced by Poland. The influx of Ukrainian nationals is advantageous for the Polish economy, but liberalising changes to German migration policy may give rise to an outflow of them. Therefore, the Polish public perhaps finds itself at the outset of a debate on whether or not Poland should introduce solutions that favour job security. It seems that guaranteeing for Ukrainians the labour market security that they miss so much could increase the probability of their staying in Poland, even if the overall level of attractiveness of the German labour market is currently beyond the reach of its Polish counterpart.

- Another relevant instrument, available to the receiving countries, is the access to social benefits. Although the notion of the free flow of workers encompasses an unrestricted access to the social security systems for all EU citizens, the number of cases of apparent violations of the aforementioned right, brought before the Court of Justice of the EU, suggests that the principle is not always fully obeyed (*Uścińska*, 2016). Furthermore, citizens of third countries have access to social benefits only according to specific regulations set by a particular receiving country (bilateral agreements are still rare). As it has been shown in this publication, access to social benefits is an important element of labour market security at times of both unemployment and transitions between jobs. Countries implementing the model based on job security should thus preferably develop a system of regulated access to social benefits for immigrants. This would guarantee them basic levels of income security while they are temporarily professionally passive. If their access to social benefits is limited, then they will be forced to make a quick decision on whether or not to move to another country or return to their country of origin. It should be emphasised in this context that looking for a new job under that model tends to take longer than under the model based on employment security (see Chapter 2). Thus, the high prevalence of periods of unemployment with minor benefits only could give rise to an outflow of immigrants, especially those who haven't already been integrated with the society of the receiving country. In countries preferring the model based on employment security, the system of social benefits accessible to immigrants does not have to be overly extensive. It is presupposed that shortly after losing a job, as a result of either a layoff or a resignation, a person will undertake new employment on terms no worse than those of the previous one. At the same time, the existence of support in the form of training and re-training for people looking for employment is necessary. The length of periods of unemployment or job seeking should be minimised in order to maintain income security.

- Receiving countries can also rely on instruments such as labour permits and thereby try to affect individual migration-related decisions. This is applicable especially in the context of states which, for various reasons, wish to limit the influx of immigrants or even encourage them to leave. For example, a country favouring job security may try to reduce the stability of employment, especially for recent newcomers. A model can be designed in accordance with which the first or even further residence and labour permits would be issued for a fixed term only. Thus, employers would be flexible in selecting the right workers. Limiting access to social benefits would perhaps have a similar effect. Benefits, for example, could be offered only to those in employment for a specified period of time, regardless of nationality or citizenship. This model is based on the assumption that there is a relationship between the taxes paid to the fiscal system and the social benefits. Yet, at the same time, such a move could contribute to the development of the 'grey zone'. States whose models are based on employment security could adopt a solution which limits the labour permit issued to third-country nationals to one employer only. This would make switching jobs practically illegal and thus risky. In this case, the model based on employment security would not be applicable in practice. On the contrary, we are dealing here with a nearly permanent bond between an employer and an employee. Once the employee quits the job, both the residence and the labour permit become invalid. As a result, the immigrant is legally obliged to return to his/her country of origin. This solution introduces a serious risk of exploiting workers and violating their rights; therefore, in democracies such a solution is usually accompanied by advanced monitoring and control routines performed by, for example, a Labour Inspectorate. A free flow of workers means that only indirect forms of pressure can be applied, for instance limiting access to training and re-training only to those workers who have worked in a respective country for a specified period of time. Training courses may also be held in the language of the receiving country.

Overall, receiving countries are in possession of a broad catalogue of instruments with which to manipulate labour market security parameters, depending on the economic and social circumstances. The range of applicable solutions obviously shrinks in the case of migrations within the EU, but even these can be influenced by means of properly designed policies. It should be assumed that factors related to labour market security should also be taken into consideration as part of the migration policy of particular countries. Labour legislation or models of social security provide instruments which, when properly used, can either stimulate or limit the influx of selected categories of immigrants. This means explicit recommendations for receiving countries. In particular, they should aim for expanding the scope of their migration policies and recognising the role played by labour legislation and social security systems. Depending on the model preferred – be it job or employment security — the measures applied may vary substantially. Nonetheless, one should be aware of their impact on the scale, the scope and the directions of migrations.

REFERENCES

Duszczyk, M. (2012). *Polska polityka imigracyjna a rynek pracy*. Warszawa: Oficyna Wydawnicza ASPRA-JR.

Hollifield, J. F. (1992). *Immigrants, markets, and states. The political economy of postwar Europe*. Cambridge, MA: Harvard University Press.

The Guardian. (2019). One in three UK firms plan for Brexit relocation, IoD says. Retrieved from https://www.theguardian.com/politics/2019/feb/01/one-three-uk-firms-activate-plans-move-operations-abroad-no-deal-brexit-iod-survey

Uścińska, G. (2016). Brexit — konsekwencje prawne i społeczne dla rynku pracy i zabezpieczenia społecznego [Brexit — legal and social consequences for labour market and security system]. *Polityka Społeczna*, *10*, 1–5.

CHAPTER 5

CONCLUSIONS
Maciej Duszczyk

For many decades, scholars have been attempting to describe the factors taken into account in the course of both making decisions to emigrate and choosing a country of destination. In the present publication, we have focused on one factor, the significance of which seems to have been increasing in recent years, namely that of labour market security. Of course, it may not seem as fundamental as imminent threats to human life, such as natural disasters, wars or famines. The main motivation behind such a type of migration as discussed here is the desire of reaching a higher level of income security and thereby accomplishing a higher standard of living for the migrant and, in some cases, her family. One's success in accomplishing such an objective depends to a great extent on her position in the labour market and on the ability to obtain a stable income. Labour market security is thus one of the factors generating incentives for people to make rational migration-related decisions.

Research carried out among Polish emigrants employed in the German and the British labour markets, among Polish university graduates who have decided to emigrate and among Ukrainian immigrants employed in Poland, has largely confirmed the conjecture that the issue of labour market security has an effect on migration-related decisions. It turns out that migrants trying to optimise their income security tend to be choosing labour markets which respond best to their expectations as regards the prevalent forms of reaching labour market security. Persons predisposed to take risks and confident about their skills are interested in emigration to countries characterised by great flexibility of their respective labour markets. For such people, both taking up the first job and finding another one is not a major issue. Therefore, they may be uninterested in signing a long-term contract with one employer, as this could hinder their potential efforts to find superior employment. We have defined this model of reaching labour market security, and thereby also income security, as 'employment security'. Such a model characterises the United Kingdom and its labour market. However, some people may prefer a model based on a high level of security defined as holding one long-term, preferably permanent, job. In this case, it is important for employees to maintain employment for long once they have obtained it. More often than not, these are persons reluctant to take risks and unconfident as to the possibility of finding another job. They may nonetheless be aware of the need for raising their professional qualifications in order to convince their employers that they are indispensable at work. We term this model as 'job security' and we argue that Germany, with its labour market, constitutes an 'ideal type' of it.

Another part of this research project concerned the migration of Ukrainians to Poland and their expectations as to labour market security. We should be aware, however, that here we are dealing with migration processes different from those analysed in the case of movement of people within the EU. In particular, there exist major differences resulting from the restricted rights granted to those migrants. Poles migrating to Germany or the United Kingdom are subject to the EU's principle of free movement of workers. This means that the vast majority of restrictions concerning labour migrations have been done away with. Ukrainians employed in Poland, on the contrary, have to apply for various kinds of permits, including entry and labour permits. As third-country citizens, they do not enjoy most of the rights which citizens of EU countries are entitled to. As a result, they have much less freedom in the choice of a country of a destination than have Polish migrants, and thus, their ability to decide where to migrate based on the preferred model of labour market security is severely limited. For Ukrainians, the choice of Poland was driven by permissive principles of entry and stay, favouring nationals of that country. At the same time, the Ukrainians interviewed emphasised explicitly that the issue of labour market security, seen in the perspective of security of earning income, was important when making migration-related decisions. Poles and Ukrainians did not differ much as regards their comparative evaluations of the labour markets in the countries of their origin and those in the countries of destination. Both nations evaluated the 'quality' of the labour market in the country where they currently stayed as much higher than in their country of origin.

Thus, in the case of labour migrations, the choice of country of destination depends, to an extent, on the particular migrant's expectations regarding the way of reaching labour market security. This is the fact that should be taken into consideration when making decisions regarding migration policy. Countries interested in the influx of immigrants who are inclined to frequent changes of employers should implement a model of labour market security based on 'employment security', whereas the countries preferring greater stabilisation and wanting to bind migrants to particular jobs should implement a model based on 'job security'.

The research presented in this publication has shown the importance of labour market security in the context of making migration-related decisions. However, numerous other issues, seeming to be equally important, have not been touched upon here. The role of trade unions, for instance, should be emphasised as well. The same applies to the support from the government administration or access to family allowances. We have to be aware that migration-related decisions are complex. The more light we throw on the various predictors of migrants' behaviour, the easier it will be to manage migration processes and, last but not least, limit the scale of the violation of both human and workers' rights, suffered by the migrating workers.

INDEX

Active labour market policy (ALMP), 87
ALMP. *See* Active labour market policy (ALMP)
Anglo-Saxon model, 9–11, 107–108

Blue-collar and low-skilled workers, 35
British labour market, 15–16, 50–51, 81, 90–91, 122–123, 147–148
British minimum wage, 84

Capitalist economies, 9, 107
Central and Eastern Europe (CEE) countries, 1–2, 11–12, 55–57
CMEs. *See* Coordinated market economies (CMEs)
Contract, types of, 88–91
Coordinated market economies (CMEs), 9, 107
characteristic, 114
Corruption, 54–55, 125–126
Cultural bias, 69–70

Economic crisis, 71–72
Economic recession, 91
Economic security, 31–32
Economic support, 138–139
Educational attainment, 37–39
Educational migration, 41
Emigration, 26–27, 119, 136–137
Emigration-immigration country, 3
Employment, 27, 29
  agencies, 54–55
  benefits, 114
  contract, 120–121
  flexible forms of, 11–12
  in Poland, 13–14
  precarious, 93–94
  protection, 29–30, 52–55, 114
  quality of, 88–91
  tenure, 139

Employment protection legislation (EPL), 52–54, 91–93
Employment Protection Legislation Index, 15–16
Employment security, 4–5, 14–15, 26–27, 30, 32–33, 50–51, 74–75, 147–148, 149–150
  flexible forms, 35–36
  model, 95–96
  term and the concept, 35–36
  "varieties of capitalism" (VoC) concept, 107–111
Enhanced employability, 35–36
Entrepreneurs, 141–142
EPL. See Employment protection legislation (EPL)
ESS. See European Social Survey (ESS)
Eurobarometer, 36–37, 96
European Economic Area, 47–48
European Social Survey (ESS), 15–16, 36–37, 68–69
European Working Conditions Survey (EWCS), 15–16, 68–69, 71–72
Eurostat, 96
  databases, 15–16

EWCS. See European Working Conditions Survey (EWCS)

Family benefits, economic support, 138–139
Financial capital, 46–47
Fixed-term employment contracts, 13–14
Flexibilisation of work, 27–28
Flexible security, 50–51
Flexicurity model, 35–36, 51, 95–96
Foreigner hiring, 53–54
Free market economic principles, 135–139

German labour markets, 15–17, 120, 122–123
Germany
  coordinated market economy, 105–106
  current employment, 77–79
  employment type, 88–90
  low-wage earners, 85–86
  median income, 83–84
  migration policy, 134–135, 141–142
  Polish employees in, 105–106
  Polish labour migrants, 111–112
  unemployment in, 79–80
"Grey zone", 143–144
  of economy, 86–87, 96
  of labour market, 13–14

Index

High job security, 77–79
High-skilled immigrants, 52
Human and social capital indicators, 37–39
Human labour, 30–31

ILO. *See* International Labour Organization (ILO)
Income security, 14–15, 31–32
 and labour market security, 119–120
Industrial democracies, 25–26
Industrial societies, 29–30
Inferior and underprivileged labour market status, 30–31
Insecurity, 27–28, 33–34
Institutional and welfare state models, 26–27
International labour market, 36
International Labour Organization (ILO), 68–69

Job insecurity, 33–34, 71–72, 109–110
Job loss, 71–72, 79
Job permanency, 114
Job placement system, 12
Job related education and training, 87–88
Job-related security, 33–34

Job security, 14–15, 31–33, 44–46, 50–51, 112–114, 126–127, 134–135, 141–142, 147–148, 149–150
 and employment security, 33–39
 level, 72–74, 105–106
 preference for, 111, 116
 socio-economic model, 79–80
 See also Employment

Labour Code, 14–15, 91
Labour Inspectorate, 143–144
Labour legislation, 136–137
 and social security systems, 144–145
Labour market arrangements, 114
Labour market instability, 88–90
Labour market security, 30, 32, 44–46
 income security and, 119–120, 120
 individual and collective goals, accomplishment, 27–33
 as migration decisions, co-determinant, 39–48
 migration goals achievement, 48–55

objective indicators, 79–82
subjective indicators, 69–79
Labour migrations, 55–57, 107–111
Labour permits, 125–126, 143–144
Labour protection legislation, 26–27, 53–54
Labour relations and employment policy, 37–39
Labour union density, 109–110
Large-scale lay-offs, 91
Liberal market economies (LMEs), 9–11, 107, 110–112
Life-time employment, 36
Lower-educated immigrants, 44–46
Low-wage earners, 85–86

Macro-level economic parameters, 37–39
Marketable qualifications and skills, 140–141
Migrants, 5–6, 51
 choice of destination country
  in-depth interviews, 119–126
  survey data analysis, 116–119
 individual decisions, 39
Migrant workers, 32–33

"Migration policy", 134
 cross-country differences, 133
 immigration policies, 131–133
 labour market security, 133
 meso- and macro-level perspectives, 131–133
 "push and pull" theory, 131–133
 receiving countries, 139–145
 sending countries, 135–139
 "welfare" magnet hypothesis, 131–133
Migration-related decisions, 14, 42, 147
 co-determinant, 39–48
 goals achievement, 48–55
 See also Labour migrations
Migration-related factor, 6–7
Minimum Wage Database, 84
Minimum wages, 84, 85, 114

National economies, VoC concept, 110–111
Native workers and labour protection legislation, 53–54
"New countries of immigration", 1–2

Index

Objective indicators, labour market security
 "frictional unemployment", 79–80
 job security, socio-economic model, 79–80
 period of fluctuation, 79–80
 public expenditures, 82, 83
 in Ukraine, 80–81
 unemployment and unemployed social expenditures, 79–82
 in United Kingdom, 81
Occupational stratification ladder, 75
Office for Foreigners, 54–55
Organisation for Economic Cooperation and Development (OECD), 68–69
 databases, 15–16

Poland
 anxiety of losing a job, 71–72
 labour market security in, 124–125
 labour migrants from, 105–106
 low-wage earners, 85–86, 88–90
 migration policy, 134–135
 security of employment, 71–72
 trade unions in, 93
 Ukrainians working in, 123–124
 unemployment in, 79–80
 wages in, 123–124
 work-related anxiety, 71–72
Polish emigrants, 3, 9–11, 147–148
Polish immigration regulations, 13–14
Polish labour market, 2–3, 96–97, 124–125
Polish labour migrants, 105–106, 111–112
 job security preference, 116, 116
 predictors of, 117
Polish-language literature, 11–12
Post-accession migration, 1–2
Post-Fordism, 27–28
Precarious employment, 93–94
"Precarious" employment, 109–110
"Precarious" migration, 14–15
"Preference for job security", 114–115, 116–119
Professional and spatial mobility, 28
Professional training and re-training, 137–138

"Push and pull factors", 6–7, 17–19, 26–27, 42, 43–44

Rate of employment, 8–9
Rate of poverty, 8–9
Receiving countries, migration policy
  entrepreneurs, 141–142
  "grey zone", 143–144
  immigrants categories, 140
  Labour Inspectorate, 143–144
  labour legislation and social security systems, 144–145
  labour permits, 143–144
  marketable qualifications and skills, 140–141
  social benefits, 142–143
  stability of employment, 140–141
  stable employment contract, 141–142
  visa policies, 139
Representation security, 31–32
Residence permits, 2–3, 125–126
Rights of foreigners, 13–14
Rights of workers, 55

Seasonal workers, 46–47
"Secure job", 70–71
Semi-legal jobs, 13–14
Sending countries, migration policy
  change of employment, 136–137
  economic support, 138–139
  emigration of people, 136–137
  free market economic principles, 135–139
  labour legislation, 136–137
  professional training and re-training, 137–138
  state of stability, 136–137
Short-term contracts, 108–109
Skill reproduction security, 31
"Social anchoring", 109–110
Social benefits, 142–143
Social indicators, 68–69
Social market economy, 11–12
Spatial mobility, 41
Stable employment, 27, 46–47, 136–137, 143–144
  contract, 141–142
State-funded benefits, 7–8, 95–96
State-funded "bonuses", 114
State Statistics Service of Ukraine (SSSU), 68–69

Index

Subjective indicators, labour market security
anxiety of losing a job, 71–72, 73
cultural bias, 69–70
degree of respondents' anxiety, 75–77
employment security, 74–75
European Working Conditions Survey, 71–72
high job security, 77–79
job insecurity, 71–72
job loss for employed persons, 71–72
occupational stratification ladder, 75
worker opinions, cross-country differences, 77–79
work performance, 75
work-related anxiety, 71–72
work-related security, 70–71
Switchable assets, 108–109

Threat of unemployment, 33–34
Trade unions, 55, 93
position, 91–93

Ukraine
immigrants, 47–48
migrants from, 125
migration policy, 134–135
Uncertainty and insecurity, 30–31
Unemployment
insurance, 55
rates, 37–39, 91, 95–96
and unemployed social expenditures, 79–82
United Kingdom
alternative (comparable) employment, 75
Anglo-Saxon model, 107–108
employment protection legislation, 91–93
employment security, 77–79
liberal market economy, 105–106
low-wage earners, 85–86
Polish labour migrants, 111–112, 115
self-perceived employment security, 74–75
trade unions in, 93
unemployment rate, 79–80

"Varieties of capitalism" (VoC) concept, 9–11, 105, 106–107
behavior of firms, 108–109
coordinated market economies (CMEs), 107

coordination mechanisms, 108–109
data and concept of analysis, 111–116
degree of "ambiguity", 110–111
and employment security, 107–111
employment security, preferences, 111
institutional features, 109–110
"institutionally coherent", 110–111
job security, preferences, 111
labour union density, 109–110
liberal market economies (LMEs), 107, 108–109
long-term survival, 108–109
national economies, 110–111
"precarious" employment, 109–110
short-term contracts, 108–109
"social anchoring", 109–110
stock market capitalization, 108–109
strategic interaction, 107–108
structural conditions, 109–110
switchable assets, 108–109
"via hierarchies and competitive market arrangements", 107–108
Visa policies, 139
Voluntary migration, 41

Wage levels, 95–96
Welfare magnet hypothesis, 14–15, 52
Welfare migration, 14–15
Welfare systems, 51–52
Workers
categories, 14, 34–35
economic well-being of, 83–87
employability, 87–88
opinions, cross-country differences, 77–79
rights and privileges, 27–28
Work permit, 17–19
Work-related anxiety, 71–72
Work-related security, 35–36, 70–71, 88–90
Work security, 31
WSI Minimum Wage, 68–69

Zero-hour contracts, 29–30, 50–51, 109–110